FROM **FRUSTRATED** TO
Fabulous

AN INSPIRATIONAL GUIDE FOR WOMEN
WHO *Dare* TO LIVE THEIR DREAMS

Praise for Amanda Jane Clarkson and *From Frustrated to Fabulous*

"*Amanda is an amazing coach and mentor* who makes me feel empowered to believe that I can achieve success in any area of my life with continued effort, support, and personal development. Amanda works a plan backwards to set a goal then chunks it down into achievable smaller steps to avoid overwhelm. She instils confidence in my ability and is so relatable with a calming and supportive presence."

—Noelene D.

"Recently I had the privilege of personal mentoring by Amanda. She took a real interest in my new start up business and helped me immeasurably. She is an excellent coach who goes above and beyond. Thanks very much Amanda."

—Julie M.

"Amanda is an amazingly dedicated individual, with real care factor for every single one of the people she mentors. She's provided so much information, time, and energy, and truly has gone above and beyond. She truly wears her heart on her sleeve and genuinely is interested in wanting everyone to succeed. I feel privileged to have met Amanda . . . she's one I will always look to as someone I can learn from and someone I aspire to. Thank you, Amanda, for everything!"

—CONNIE B.

"Amanda has enabled me to transform my life and I will be forever grateful. Amanda understood my business idea and provided alternative viewpoints for strategy, marketing, and networking. I've become more organized and focus-oriented with a positive outlook. Not only has my business become more successful, Amanda's mentoring has had a major impact on my life, including my relationships with my family and friends. My newfound confidence has had such an impact, and this was the biggest surprise for me."

"Now, I live my life on my terms. Amanda assisted me to empower myself in ways I had not thought of, both in business and my personal life. Negative beliefs that were holding me back now are banished. I've become laser-focused, all doubts have been crushed thanks to Amanda. It has been an amazing journey.

"Amanda's coaching, questioning, and challenging combined with listening skills teased out the most important issues and Amanda helped me to become goal-oriented. Problems are not problems now—I know how to ultimately action a solution.

"I cannot thank Amanda enough. It's her holistic approach to business and life in general that inspires me. Her no-nonsense approach, her trustworthiness, and most of all her honesty.

"I have a saying that I live by: *Just do it.* Don't think, don't second-guess yourself, just do it."

—ROSIE C.

"Feel the fear and do it anyway. As a result, I now have a seven-figure income and growing! This is the number one lesson I have learnt from Amanda Clarkson, who has been my mentor for the last eight years. Amanda already had the results and the lifestyle I was striving for, so I knew she was the *real deal.* A hugely successful business woman who absolutely loved what she was doing and loved sharing with others how to achieve the same results. The investment has been worth every single cent because now I am living my dream and earning an income that I didn't believe possible.

"I feel enormous gratitude to Amanda every day and if you were ever thinking about finding a mentor who is warm, truthful, and real, then I can think of no one better to guide you on your own journey to success."

—CATHY Y.

"I sat glued to my seat while I watched and learnt. Amanda has such presence on stage and was able to explain everything in a way that was easy to understand. She has such a fun way about her and is so dedicated to helping you achieve your goals. I would not be where I am today without her guidance. To anyone thinking about using Amanda as a mentor, I could not recommend her more highly. She is very approachable and is so dedicated to helping you achieve your goals."

—ANNIE L.

"Amanda is an amazing mentor who is passionate about her students' success. We would not have continued on this journey if it wasn't for Amanda's positive outlook, her *go get it* attitude, and her ability to help her students understand and feel confident to strive towards and achieve their dreams. Thank you, Amanda for being by our side during this crazy journey. You're such a beautiful person and an inspiration to us! We highly recommend Amanda as a mentor if you're looking to change your life!"

—JULIE AND ADRIAN

"As a book collaborator and editor, and as a student of self-development for most of my life, it seems very little surprises me—in fact I can be critical, even cynical about self-help books, unless I find one with true, modern value and an ability to genuinely reach a particular market. After reading *Frustrated to Fabulous*, I have to say it's both timely and timeless for the genre, and I (while not a lady) derived great value from it— in fact it has had a profound effect on my thinking and my own vision for my future. I was very happily surprised! I think the difference is that Amanda has truly and honestly achieved the things we all dream of without defining success as *stuff*, but as freedom, experiences, and most of all, precious personal development. It's also that Amanda (if you read her story) demonstrates her innate desire and nurturing character for helping others achieve the stellar success she has herself. It's all in the book, and it all comes from both her head and her heart. Thank you, Amanda for writing this!"

—RODNEY MILES

Editing and book design, *Frustrated to Fabulous*

"Thank you, Amanda! Your energy to light up a room is awesome and the knowledge you shared was just amazing!"

—MARILYN W.

FROM **FRUSTRATED** TO
Fabulous

AN INSPIRATIONAL GUIDE FOR WOMEN
WHO *Dare* TO LIVE THEIR DREAMS

AMANDA JANE CLARKSON

LIVE
NOW
BOOKS

Copyright ©2018 by Amanda Jane Clarkson
All rights reserved.
Published by LIVE NOW BOOKS

No part of this book may be reproduced in any manner without written permission except in the case of brief quotations embodied in critical articles and reviews.

Although the author and publisher have made every effort to ensure that the information in this book was correct at press time, the author and publisher do not assume and hereby disclaim any liability to any party for any loss, damage, or disruption caused by errors or omissions, whether such errors or omissions result from negligence, accident, or any other cause. Forms and agreements are included for your information only.

For information about special discounts for bulk purchases or author interviews, appearances, and speaking engagements please contact:

info@gdaygorgeous.com

First Edition

Cover design by Cris Edwards
Editing, interior design, and production by Rodney Miles:
www.rodneymiles.com

Dedication

I DEDICATE THIS BOOK to you and every woman who dares to dream of a better future and who knows deep down she deserves it.

If you are...

- Determined to commit to an exciting new future full of fun, freedom, and fabulous new adventures,
- Want to be inspired by a mentor who has travelled the road before you,
- And if you want to save yourself time and money and learn from my mistakes and take advantage of my expensive lessons,

then *welcome*.

This book is dedicated to you.

FREE GIFT!

THIS BOOK is just the beginning of our time together. I have another special gift for you, gorgeous—a gift that will clarify the lessons in this book and give you a better idea on how to live your life by design, not default. Introducing my...

LIVE NOW Freedom Formula
Web Class

During this online presentation, I go deeper into my LIVE NOW Freedom Formula, so you too can transform your life and live with more confidence, choice, and freedom. Based on over two decades of life lessons and tens of thousands of dollars invested in the best mentors from around the world, this web class gives you the power to take control of your life and design the life you truly deserve. You'll discover...

- The easiest way to banish negative self-talk and fill your life with hope and joyful expectations! (You'll see how to let go and love yourself for who you are.)

- How to stay on track every day no matter what life throws at you. (Never get overwhelmed again.)

- The simple exercise that turns your dreams into reality. (This is an important part of your transformation.)

- How to feel empowered every minute of every day. (Gives you confidence and certainty in an uncertain world.)

- An important element in your success journey you must master. (Makes you unstoppable.)

- How to be effective not just busy. (A powerful exercise that gets things done.)

- Unlock the power of your mind and take control of your thoughts, habits, and actions. (This is where your true transformation begins.)

And so much more! So let's continue this grand new adventure together. This web class is the perfect companion to this book and gives you extra clarity on transforming your life. To register for this FREE web class, simply go to this link:

www.gdaygorgeous.com/webclass

"We are always getting ready to live, but never living."
—RALPH WALDO EMERSON

CONTENTS

Dedication xi

FREE BONUS! xii

Prologue: Fabulous xix

Introduction: Freedom 1

PART ONE 7

[1] Moving Out 8

[2] Pie Princess 25

[3] Video Store 34

[4] Get Down and Give Me Twenty! 42

[5] The Cat, the Rat, and the Two Dressed in White 62

[6] G'Day L.A.! 79

[7] Careful What You Wish For 94

[8] The Big Stage 117

[9] Cups of Concrete...............................132

[10] The Curtain Comes Down but Dreams Never Die 152

PART TWO 175

[11] Your LIVE NOW Freedom Formula 176

    L, Love and Let Go.............................184

    I, Imagine What is Possible............................189

    V, Visualize Success 196

    E, Empower Your Mind, Body, Spirit 200

    N, Never Quit.................................208

    O, Opportunity.................................212

    W, Willing, Whatever it Takes 215

[12] The Butterfly effect.............................222

About the Author...236

Acknowledgements 247

Prologue:

Fabulous

September 22, 2018

YESTERDAY, six of us, and friends of almost 20 years, sailed a catamaran we had hired for two weeks into IOS (Isle of Ios, Greece), a quaint and happy place where locals are welcoming. This dream trip had been on our wish list for a while and after two years of careful planning, we were living what was once just an idea over a long, fun lunch. The night before we dined at probably the most stunning ocean-view restaurant I've ever been in, "Grandmas." The warm sea breeze, the company of fabulous friends, and the food—Michelin star-rated, OMG—we ate, drank, and laughed like there was no tomorrow. It was an experience I'll never forget, with friends I'll cherish forever.

This morning we arrived in breathtaking Santorini ready to explore, take photos, and share another day of adventure… Bring it on I say!

Keep your dreams alive, friends. They *can* come true. Enjoy, and I'll see you soon!

Introduction: Freedom

"Twenty years from now you will be more disappointed by the things that you didn't do than by the ones you did do, so throw off the bowlines, sail away from safe harbor and catch the trade winds in your sails. Explore. Dream. Discover."

—MARK TWAIN.

"IS THIS ALL there is?" I cried out in despair. I was in my early 40s, flat broke, and living in a cheap motel room that had seen better days. I had tried, and I had failed, and I'd lost a small fortune in the process. I felt embarrassed and ashamed. I forced a smile, pretending everything was fine, while deep inside I was slowly falling apart. Yet a flicker of hope remained, like a glowing ember that refuses to die. I knew there was more to life than fear and survival. There was more to life than frustration and desperation. I had tasted a small sample of the bounty of life and I was determined to taste some more! Little did I know then that within a few short years my life would change, and I would be living my dreams every single day. It wasn't always easy. It wasn't always fun. There were many challenges along the way. That story and those lessons are what I share with you in this book, so you too can go from frustrated to fabulous, so you too can live a life full of abundant joy and laughter.

Do you ever feel frustrated with your life? Do you ever get so overwhelmed you just want to scream? And do you ever feel there's more to life than your daily grind and that you were made for bigger things? If so, you're not alone. Millions of women around the world feel the same way. They tell me it's like they're treading water. Every day they get more frustrated, more dissatisfied, and instead of springing out of bed each morning they dread the start of the new day. And as the years roll on by, they feel like they're running out of time. They get more frustrated, tired, and unhappy. It's a downward spiral.

But it doesn't have to be this way.

You can live a life full of fun and adventure. You can experience your goals, live your wildest dreams and taste the freedom of a remarkable life full of laughter. And believe it or not, you've already started on your new, exciting journey by picking up this book. You see girlfriend, there is a formula to getting what you want in life. A formula that lets you live your life by design, not by default. And it's this formula, what I call my LIVE NOW Freedom Formula, that I share with you inside this book. This is not your everyday self-help book from someone with no life experience who has read a few books, copied the ideas, and compiled them into a new book.

Not even close.

I'm a woman in my fifties. I left school (and home) at 16 and since then I've had 33 different jobs and started 14 businesses from scratch (not all successful as you'll soon see). This guidebook is based on my *very* real-life experiences. I've had my share of shitty and frustrating times, and learnt life lessons by facing them head-on, somehow getting through and sticking to the formula I'll share with you soon. You'll see my setbacks, heartaches, wins, losses, lessons, and everything in between, in order to get a life I truly love living in every way imaginable. I know what it's like to be broke, alone, in tears, not knowing where to turn and feeling absolutely helpless. And I know what it's like to stand on stage in front of thousands of people and share my story of hope and transformation. I know what it's like to live in my dream home, to travel the world, to mentor and inspire women from all corners of the globe and take them from frustrated to fabulous.

By sharing my story—the good, the bad, and the ugly—I hope to inspire you to live your life with purpose, with passion, without fear, and without apology. And by giving you my LIVE NOW Freedom Formula I'll be giving you the guidance you need to create an extraordinary life full of abundance. No matter where you are in life, no matter which area of your life you want to improve or transform or what your goals and dreams look like, the Freedom Formula gives you the answers, so you can experience all of the wonderful things you so thoroughly deserve.

You'll find this book a fun and easy read. Each chapter contains my story and the lessons I've learnt from facing every challenge head-on. And to fast-track your own success, I close each chapter with "Frustrated to Fabulous Life Lessons" and action steps. These include gifts and lessons for you to gain from. Be sure to keep your journal close so you can keep notes to shortcut the time between where you are now to where you want to be. These life lessons are universal. Read them carefully my friend, they are potent and can give you the life I know you want, if you truly want it bad enough.

To finish up the book, I give you my LIVE NOW Freedom Formula. This way, you can live your life by design, not by default. Use this formula to transform all areas of your life beginning exactly where you are right now. You will see that becoming successful in any area of your life doesn't have to mean pain or huge financial investment. You can EMPOWER and CHANGE your life with intelligent, proven steps by making small, daily shifts in your thinking and actions just as I did. As a result of working harder *on myself* than *in* any business, job or career I've ever had, I humbly share that I have become self-made, empowered, and fulfilled. More importantly, I *like* the person I've become throughout my journey and every day I feel grateful and excited to be alive as I live my life by design, not by default and certainly not in desperation.

Frustrated to Fabulous

Now, it's your turn.

Turn the page and begin this exciting new journey with me.

AMANDA JANE CLARKSON

PART ONE

FROM FRUSTRATED TO FABULOUS

[1] Moving Out

"The future belongs to those who see possibilities before they become obvious."

—John Sculley.

I WAS ONLY 14 years of age the day I walked up the side lane of our neat, red, brick home after school and discovered my whole bedroom—all of my clothes and prized possessions—strewn over Mum's manicured backyard lawn. We hadn't been broken into, or anything like that. It was Mum's way of dealing with her own stress if I hadn't tidied up the bedroom I shared with my two sisters properly or put my clothes away after she'd washed them. As usual she was clearly furious about something I'd done, but I had no idea what her problem was. Standing there staring at the mess on the lawn, feelings of anger, shame, resentment, and even hatred towards her washed over me like big waves as tears welled in my eyes. In that exact moment, I knew I wanted to leave home the first chance I could. I was over living by Mum's harsh and sometimes brutal rules.

I had about $20 (which was a lot back then) I had saved from all the chores and jobs I did around the house and those for our neighbours, which was stashed in my special black-and-gold lockable box I had hidden under my mattress. Thank God she didn't know where I hid it, or she'd probably have tossed it in her rage. I barely made it over to where my stuff had landed when she started yelling at me from the kitchen which overlooked the perfect back yard we played in.

"Start picking up your things and this time put them away properly, or else!" She said.

"Yeah, yeah," I muttered under my breath, "Here we go again! Shut up, you old bag. I can't stand you. I hate you."

These and many other wicked thoughts filled my mind, as tears rolled down my face, knowing she'd probably give me a *hiding* soon as I got inside. Mum was meticulous and proud about her house, the yard, cleanliness, and neatness. Seriously, you could eat food off the polished tiled kitchen floors, it was that spotless. Everything in our home had its it place and things had to be done exactly as Mum liked, otherwise we'd feel the pain of her fast palm across the back of our heads, or wherever she could reach, as we tried to duck and weave away from her. She had a fast hand

and back then it was just the way we kids were disciplined. "Like it or lump it," as she'd say.

It was the early 1970s and I was the middle child of five kids living at home with Mum, Dad, and our pets in a town named Launceston, in Tasmania. In most ways we were the average Australian working-class family. My parents did their best to give us a great childhood—good schools, a nice home, commitment to our after-school activities, and awesome family camping trips. Mum was a mentally strong woman, who had lost two dads in the Second World War, and my dad was one of nine children. They grew up tough-minded and knew how to take care of themselves and others. They toiled and worked from sunup, to sundown, day-in, day-out, like most other mum's and dad's I knew. It was just the way it was.

Dad was a solid plasterer and had his own contracting business. He worked with his hands and was extremely talented and hard-working. Like most Australians at the time, he wanted to pay off the mortgage and looked forward to a better life. Mum did the bookwork, ran our home, took care of us five kids and even found time to cook for other families in the street for extra income. On top of that, Mum would care for underprivileged welfare kids while also running a busy childcare centre for babies and toddlers up to five years of age, with her sister Patsy. Every two to three months running, a different young boy or girl would come to our home and live with us for around three months. They were welfare children that came from underprivileged homes and weren't well-cared for by their own parents for all sorts of reasons.

Being a young girl at the time, seeing their sad little faces from being ill-treated by adults made me cry a lot and I always wanted to cuddle them till their pain went away. They were so young, still in nappies and although Mum had five of her own kids to take care of, somehow, she found it in her heart to open our home to them. Mum made it mostly *my* job to take care of these little ones and love them as if they were my own and even though I was young at the time, I found it easy and natural to do what was needed. She taught me what to do, and always watched over me to make sure I gave each one all the love and care they craved for and needed. Things like bathing, feeding, playing, reading, and bringing little smiles to their eyes was my payoff. I never complained about my role much and even though I was only 12 when Mum started letting these kids come and live with us, I knew even then that our mostly loving family environment was impacting those kids' lives in so many positive ways. They all grew to love us as much as we did them. And even though Mum had a fast hand and a bad temper at times, she also had a warm and loving heart for others, and us kids. That was amazing for me to watch and learn from as a role model. I can't imagine the stress she must have been under at times and without her generosity and kindness, who knows where those underprivileged kids may have ended up?

There were often six kids, Mum and Dad and our pets, all living in a three-bedroom home with one bathroom and one toilet. It wasn't easy, but if we complained, Mum would come down on us like a ton of bricks. She reminded us how lucky we were to have a warm bed, food on the table, and parents who took care of us. We shut up and learned to live with her decisions.

It was never a good idea to argue with Mum.

My little brother Kristian, who is ten years younger than me, would have to give his bunkbed up if it was a little boy living with us, or if it were a girl, she'd share my bunk bed with me. When Mum first started bringing these other kids home, Kristian was still practically a baby himself. Mum was so busy with so much going on, I spent as much time helping her bring him up, as I did the welfare kids. To this day, he and I have a special bond and he always says that I was like a mum to him more than a sister.

I'd often skip school (which I hated anyway) to work with mum and Aunty Patsy at their childcare centre, which opened from 8 a.m. till about 2 p.m. I'd help out with feeding babies, changing nappies, playing, and caring with little kids who were too young for school. I loved it because I was used to having other people's kids live with us. It was all normal and back then, it's just the way it was. We'd draw on the blackboard, colour, and stick pictures onto big pieces of cardboard. We'd play in the sandpit, feed them morning tea and lunch, and then pop them down for a nap, till their parents came to pick them up by 2 p.m. when the doors closed. Never once did Mum complain with all that she'd taken on. Neither did I. It wasn't worth it.

I grew up fast because I had to. I was still too young to move out of home, but I thought about it every day. I couldn't wait to get my own place and be my own boss. It was only a dream then, but it kept me going.

FRUSTRATED TO FABULOUS

Even though I had the responsibility of taking care of other people's vulnerable kids, to me they were so adorable. All they wanted was love and nurturing which was easy for me. These kids soon became a part of our family unit and as each day passed, it was as though they'd lived with us for years. I grew to love all those little cherubs in my own way and as each left after about three months to go back to where they came from, I always cried and pined for them as though they were my own.

Such was life, as they say.

Sunday was church day. We all had to attend—It was Nan's only rule and believe me, there was no getting out of it. Nan was a quiet, holy woman who'd seen too much pain in her life. She didn't say too much. She usually kept quiet and waited hand-and-foot on Pop who ruled the roost with an iron fist and had a temper to match. He was a warfie[1] boss, and back then, no one crossed him. Every one of his nine kids and grandkids were shit-scared of him, me and Nan included. Nan spent her days cooking and doting on her kids, their spouses, and dozens of grandkids. She'd often go out the back of her house, chase down a chicken, cut its head off on a big wooden block, pluck it, clean it, and cook it all in a few hours. Looking at her you'd never think she had it in her, but she was tough on the inside and her life wasn't easy by any stretch of the imagination.

I hated the cold, wooden pews in church, but I loved the beautiful stained-glass windows. I'd stare up

---

[1] Australian longshoreman, wharf laborer, or anyone who works on the wharves. —urbandictionary.com

at them hoping the sermon would end soon. I wanted to get back to Nan's place because Sunday meant homemade hot scones, jam, and cream at her house after church. The thought of it was enough to comfort me through the painful time sitting in the wintery cold, which I didn't like one bit. But I did love when the big hessian (wicker, offering) basket got handed around, so I could take a peek inside to see how much money had been thrown in. It was magical to my limited mind. Where was all that money going? What did they do with it all? All those dollar bills and silver coins, along with the little brown shiny ones and two-cent pieces. I wished it were my job to count the money. Nan would give me a penny and I'd throw it in the big hessian basket at church, dreaming of the day when I'd have a big basket of my own money, real money I could put into my cash register, not just play money.

Growing up I'd always dreamed of becoming a millionaire. Back in the 1970s the idea of becoming rich—and a million dollars was way more money back then—seemed grand and exciting like in the movies, not that I'd ever met a millionaire. Mum and Dad were making enough money to give us a good upbringing, but the subject of money and how to make it was never a topic of conversation. Like most people, we were taught to go to school, get a good job, and retire on government retirement benefits.

Yeah right.

One of my favourite toys when I was younger was my small red and green metal cash register. It had little round buttons with numbers on them that I'd push down, and it would make a *cha-ching* sound. My sister Kylie and I used to play a game. She'd be the housewife

FRUSTRATED TO FABULOUS

with three kids and I'd be the shopkeeper. I'd accept fake money (from the monopoly set) or even hand-written checks that we'd make up. I'd take all the groceries out of Mum's cupboard and set up shop in the backyard and we'd play for hours.

Growing up, I'd tell anyone who'd listen to me that one day I was going to be successful and make enough money so I could do anything I wanted, travel the world, and help other people, too. No one took me seriously. In fact, statements like those were usually met with laughter, a sneer, and comments like, "As if. You're too stupid. You'll never be a millionaire. Who do you think you are?" I didn't care, I just believed that somehow, some day, it would happen. The jeers and the torment carried on throughout my teenage years, but I kept at it, always finding ways to make pocket money.

The dream of leaving home, making something of myself and being free was alive and well. *One of these days, I'd show 'em all, and then who'd be laughing, eh?*

Cooking, cleaning, picking fruit, babysitting, spinning wool, feeding our dozen or more pets, shopping for others, buying and selling candy back to my brothers and sisters, massaging Dad's tired hands and feet after a long day on a building site—you name it, I did it. My best friend Tracey who lived at the end of the street liked the idea of making money too, so we started a little sweet shop together. We called it "Betsy's Sweet Shop." Betsy was the name of the street I lived in. We'd ride our bikes to the local shop, which was few miles away, buy as many sweets as we could afford, bag them up, and go door-knocking together. I saved every penny I got my hands on, stashing it in my

15

little black-and-gold lockable box, hidden safely under my mattress.

And moving out was always on my mind.

All the while, my friends and family laughed and poked fun at me. *So what!* I thought. I was used to it by then. Nothing fazed me.

One day I got into massive trouble. My older sister Carmel was a runner at national representation level. One day she snuck into the kitchen after I'd spent nearly all day baking Anzac oat biscuits[2] to sell back to my own family and around the neighbourhood. I knew how many I had *exactly*. I was going to make a tidy profit after selling out, which would take a couple of days. But Carmel snuck into the kitchen while I was distracted at the stove and grabbed a big pile of them, shoving them into her bag. I spun around in time to catch her in the act and I was so mad, I instinctively picked up my wooden rolling pin and took a swing at her. The rolling pin handle got her right on the tip of her elbow and it broke her bone just under the joint.

I don't know who was more surprised. I didn't mean to hurt her, I was just angry and wanted to teach her a lesson. She was stealing the profits from my biscuit business, but really, she meant no harm. But it was too late. She had a broken elbow and I knew what was coming for me. I felt the blood drain from my face

---

[2] An Anzac biscuit is a sweet biscuit, popular in Australia and New Zealand, made using rolled oats, flour, sugar, butter, golden syrup, baking soda, boiling water, and desiccated coconut. —Wikipedia

FRUSTRATED TO FABULOUS

as she let out an almighty squeal of pain that got Mum running to the kitchen.

That was it.

I got the biggest hiding of my life and Carmel was rushed to hospital to get her arm put in plaster. I bawled my eyes out for hours and never got to live that one down. Thankfully Carmel forgave me, and she healed quickly to return to her running, but she never, ever stole my biscuits again, and I never took a swing at her again.

The following summer, I turned 16, and all I wanted to do was leave home and get my own place. We didn't have any welfare kids that were living with us at the time, so I wanted to make my move. Mum and Dad didn't bat an eyelid when I told them I was moving out, so one Saturday morning, I filled my little sky-blue 1967 VW beetle with everything I owned, which wasn't much, and headed for the hills of Trevallyn, Launceston. I moved into a tiny granny flat by myself, which was underneath another family's house about ten miles away. I loved it because finally I had my own space, including my own bathroom and toilet, which was a treat. I could do what I wanted and focus on my own life. I went from job to job in search of fulfillment. I hated every one of them after about six months, always feeling flat and caged-in. Nothing seemed to excite me after a couple of months doing the same thing every day. I was bored easily.

People couldn't believe or accept I wouldn't stay in a job where I was constantly frustrated because I didn't enjoy it. I had no real guidance from Mum and Dad, they were way too busy and besides, Mum would always say, "Don't whine about your job to me Amanda. If you don't like it, do something about it or shut up." So I did. And looking back, while her advice wouldn't fit with some, it was perfect for me. By forcing me to think and make conscious and better decisions for myself, she was preparing me mentally for a life I could design any way I wanted it. So, I'd resign and move on to the next and the next.

At one stage, I was working three part-time jobs. I was twenty-five years of age by now. I was selling advertising for the local *Examiner* newspaper up till lunchtime. It was a commission role, but I did quite well and enjoyed the office atmosphere mostly, but I didn't like the office politics. At 12:30 p.m. I'd change into my old clothes and run about a mile to the local gravel yard. My job was to operate a big yellow front-end loader. Massive trucks would pull into the yard and I'd fill them with dirt or gravel. When I wasn't busy filling trucks, I'd clean up the yard, moving sand, dirt, and gravel to different bays making sure everything was neat and in its right place. The truck drivers were all nice to me. I suppose they had no choice because we were the main gravel yard in town so all they cared about was getting in and out as fast as they could. It was such a cool job, one that I actually loved at the time!

The owner Toby and his partner Rich would sit in their small on-site office drinking coffee, talking, and doing the books, keeping an eye on me in case I needed help. We were pretty good friends too. Toby was the boyfriend of my younger sister Kylie at the time. At 5 p.m. I'd get a lift home with one of the guys. I'd quickly shower, change, and walk to the local pub. There I'd run the bar, serve food, operate the TAB betting counter, clean up, listen to lies, stories, gossip and laughter from our customers, till closing time at 9:30 p.m. I'd get home around 10 p.m., fall into bed, and do it all again the next day. I was on the hamster wheel six days a week, saving as much money as I could, because I'd decided I wanted to leave Tasmania. I was ready to grow my wings and expand my universe. I was so focused on getting what I wanted and six months later, I sold every possession I owned. It was time to see what life I could make for myself.

I displayed every item I owned on the front lawn of the house I shared with three other friends. Everything sold by lunchtime, including my beloved 1967 sky-blue Volkswagen Beetle. I didn't own much, but I had bigger, grander adventures in mind. I'd saved enough money to buy a ticket and move to the Gold Coast, Queensland, where it was sunny, warm, and full of promise. Mum and Dad had moved there a few years earlier after selling up everything too. At the time they didn't consider what us older kids wanted to do. They said we could do what we pleased. When they left, only my younger brother Kristian went with them. Within two weeks of landing in Queensland with just a big cardboard box of belongings, I settled into a new flat on the Gold Coast where I believed I'd found paradise. I bought a bike and easily found work near where I lived. In fact, within the first two years I had four different jobs. I was still frustrated with my life and into my *thirty-third job* (no, not a typo!) when I finally realized a *job* was never going to satisfy the burning desire I had within myself, to live life on my own terms.

One morning I looked at myself in the mirror and said, "Girlfriend, it's time for a nice big cup of *concrete* and to learn to stand on your own two feet!"

FRUSTRATED TO FABULOUS LIFE LESSONS

Okay Gorgeous, it's time to make a nice cuppa, take yourself and your journal to a quiet area for 15 minutes and write in *detail* your top three-to-five take-away *a-has* from my story so far and from the lessons that follow below.

Be Bold.
Be Courageous.
Be Fabulous!

This chapter of my young life was to bring many new and challenging growth lessons. I was always the odd one out because I wanted a different life than "the norm." And no matter how hard they laughed at me, pulled me down, or told me I wasn't worthy, I had to ignore them till I got away from negative influence. Sure, my feelings were often crushed but I couldn't live the lie. The burning desire inside of me outweighed the jeers and sneers of others and I knew I'd find the nerve some way to pursue my dreams. I was surrounded by so many *pullers* (people who love to pull you down and keep you small) I literally had to *move to another state* to get away from them. Still, for years I blamed my mistakes, failures, and excuses on others, creating pathetic stories that kept me trapped in a cul-de-sac with no way out other than to stop and head in a new direction.

For years I blamed my parents, family, teachers, and outside influences for how my life was turning out. Back then, I didn't have the answers nor the tools, but I realized one thing—it was time to grow up and let go of the past, time to let go of the anger, resentment, and frustration I felt towards my mother knowing deep-down she was doing her very best with all the tools she had at the time. She was a powerful woman in her own way, but so was I, and I could learn to take the best of what she taught and gave me and change my destiny forever, and maybe even the destiny of others. The disempowering thoughts I had as result of my childhood needed to be weeded out and replaced with a fresh garden of possibility. I wanted to focus on the present and get on with my life, and I was willing to keep searching for the answers till I found them.

I get that it's a hard pill to swallow, taking responsibility for where you're at in life. Why weren't we taught life success lessons in schools for God's sake? Why are we left to figure the most important lessons of life out for ourselves? I'd made up my mind that nothing or no one would stop me from finding the answers to the freedom I was seeking. I was ready for my new grand adventure in life.

Are you?

Because if you feel like the merry-go-round of your life is spinning out of control, maybe like me back then, you haven't truly committed to, or accepted that it is *your* responsibility, and if you desire change in certain areas of your life, it's up to *you* to take the right action because no one but you is here to make your life happy.

Does this make sense?

And if you are relating to my story in any way and the lessons I share make you squirm or feel uncomfortable, don't worry, I get you! I was no different. It was hard to face the truth, but I had to in the end because my dreams were bigger than my ego. I had no choice but to look inside of myself for the answers I'd been seeking in others and the outside world. I was miserable at the time, but enough was enough. You see the only way you can know how your life will look in the future is to *plan* for it and take the necessary steps to getting there. Take some big, bold chances and see what you're made of.

And looking back now, I'm so grateful for my childhood, although some would say it was tough. It was, but on the flip-side, I became more daring, I took more chances. I became open to opportunity, forgiveness, hope, and adventure in my younger years, instead of waiting till it was too late and I was too scared.

Are *you* open to opportunity, forgiveness, hope, and a new chapter in your life, a better life on your own terms instead of someone else's? Look back at your life's great tapestry now and write down all the ways you know you're looking on the outside of yourself to

FRUSTRATED TO FABULOUS

take the blame for things not working out for you, in each area of your life.

Who are you mad at?

Who are you angry, resentful, or even hateful towards?

Is it yourself or others?

Are you holding onto stories from the past that cannot and will let you move forward?

Girlfriend, do you think it's time to step into your inner strength and find a way to let go of your past if it's not serving you?

Is it time to practice forgiveness in your heart for yourself and others?

Are you ready to begin your own inner-child healing process to make way for an empowered, loving woman to emerge, as I was?

I understand it's a work in progress, however if you make the commitment today as I did all those years ago, your life can and will take on new meaning, more joy, and more fulfillment in all ways.

Be the change that you want to see in yourself and others starting today and know that you are worthy of a life by design and not default, in every way imaginable. You see, although I haven't met you personally yet, if we ever get the chance (and I hope we do through my online G'day Gorgeous community), I'd love to hear your story and what you were taught growing up.

I'll bet we have much in common.

I believe in you girlfriend. If I can make the big decisions that helped me begin to get my life in order and focus on my goals and dreams, then so can you.

I'm here to inspire and open your heart to believing that you can be truly fulfilled and happy in any area of your life you choose. It'll take commitment from you. It'll take courage, guts, and determination.

Do you have the willpower?

And yes, life will certainly throw some interesting lessons that all play a role and test you to see who you are and who you're becoming. My friend, it's just like the magnificent story of how a cocoon transforms in to a beautiful butterfly, it's time to transform your life one step at a time, grow your wings of inspiration, and never glance backwards. Dare to live with courage and fearlessness, and beginning today, begin to transform the result of any area of your life that you're not happy with.

I am here with you every step of the way in heart and spirit. I've done it, so you can you.

Are you *still* willing?

If so, keep reading my friend. You will find your answers and salvation emerge as we stay on our merry way ☺

FREE GIFT

www.gdaygorgeous.com/webclass

[2] Pie Princess

"Success is about dedication. You may not be where you want to be or do what you want to do when you're on the journey, but you've got to be willing to have vision and foresight that leads you to an incredible end."

—Usher

IT WAS A MONDAY afternoon at 4 p.m. on a warm, late summers day when I flopped down onto the soft, freshly-cut green grass in the backyard of the small townhouse I was renting, bawling my eyes out uncontrollably, feeling sorry for myself wondering how my life had gotten to this. I was thirty years young and life was supposed to be good. I was supposed to be going places but the only place I was going was to *hell*. Or at least that's how it seemed to me. It was the end of the first day of my brand-new business, which I'd dreamed of starting for the past year. And in that moment feeling alone, embarrassed, tired, and totally freaked out, I realized I'd made one of the biggest mistakes of my life. I had started this business for *all* the wrong reasons. I hated it already and it was only my first day! There was no turning back. I had responsibilities—*big* responsibilities—and business people I couldn't let down. As I sat on that lawn sobbing like a child, I felt waves of dread wash over me.

What the frigging hell have I just done? I asked myself in sheer panic. My answer was simply, *Suck it up princess. You got what you asked for and now you have no choice but to live with it!* The little, nagging voice inside my head was telling me I was stupid. Telling me I was a failure, just like I'd failed almost every subject at school. *What an idiot!* My negative inner chatter wouldn't shut up.

The business was a mobile food truck and I was known as the Pie Princess. It had been a dream of mine for a year before I got the courage to start it. I bought the food truck, decked it out (all on credit card) and by door-knocking and sheer determination, I secured twenty factories and nine building sites within a week that agreed to have me turning up to their site, two times a day to feed the hungry men and women. I was on my way. I had a plan—a good plan, or so I'd thought. I wanted to start that business to make money, have fun, and hopefully to meet a good-looking guy. I was single and ready to settle down. I was thirty years of age and didn't want to be left on the shelf, as they say. My business plan was absurd, but it sounded good at the time.

After that first day when the remorse of what I'd created kicked in, and I'd cried myself dry, I pulled myself together, gave myself a good, hard kick in the ass, and headed back to the make-shift commercial (and illegal) kitchen Dad had rigged up for me in my two-car garage. The only reason I got away with not being evicted was because each day I'd cook a big tray of home-baked bacon and egg pie for the business complex managers. It was their favourite and it must have been good because they turned a blind-eye to my little business that should never have been operating on that premises. Day after day, Monday to Friday, like a rat on a wheel, I'd get out of bed at 3:30 a.m. and prepare enough food for up to three hundred customers. Then I'd drive to twenty-nine different locations twice a day, serve, smile, banter, and be as happy as I could pretend to be.

After a year, I outgrew the little makeshift kitchen in my garage, so I moved into a small industrial shop. Even though it was better for my business, I was working harder and harder trying to keep up with the growth and the growing bills that came with it. On the outside I was all smiles and laughter, but on the inside, I was tired, pissed off, angry with myself for being stuck running a business I had zero desire for, and running myself ragged.

Life sucked.

Each afternoon I'd get back to the kitchen around 2:30 p.m. I'd clean and wash the truck, spend three more hours preparing and cooking food for the next day, then go to the markets to stock up again. I'd get home at around 5 p.m. absolutely exhausted, hoping my truck would blow up or something, so I'd have a good excuse to quit. But I didn't. I just kept going. I'd ask myself every day, *Is this it?* And the answer back was always the same: *You don't know anything else. It's too late now, and you can't let your loyal customers down. Anyway, what would your friends, family, and customers think of you if you just quit? They'd laugh at you and call you a loser! Just suck it up, Princess! What a joke!*

Nice.

On top of that, there were many weeks I couldn't even meet the rent. I had lots of bills and not being a good businesswoman back then, I either spent all the money or gave it away. For some reason I had a blockage around money and didn't feel worthy enough to learn how to handle it properly, let alone invest and grow it. I had a lady helping me three days a week. I knew she was helping herself to the till, but I was so fed up and tired, I didn't even have the guts to confront her. I was too scared she'd quit if I said anything and then I'd really be up shit creek! At one point when I couldn't pay the rent, which was $250 a week, I negotiated with my landlord, Geoff, and he agreed to let me off the rent for a few weeks in return for home-cooked hot, roast chickens. No, this is not a typo! I actually used to cook them in my shop and he was kind enough to see it was his only option. I had no money, so fresh roast chickens a couple times a week was his best option.

And after three long, frustrating, and unhappy years of slogging it out, complaining and feeling sorry for myself, something great happened. (No, the pie van

FRUSTRATED TO FABULOUS

didn't blow up, though I wish it would have.) I actually met a guy. He was different from anyone else I'd ever been out with. He made me laugh so much I'd be in tears and it felt good. His name is Matt and he was the one for me. We'd hang out every opportunity we could. We'd just have fun and laugh, and I'd forget about the business for a while. It was good medicine and it worked. My business plan had actually worked, come to think of it ;-)

Matt was one of my customers from a building site and we met one night at a live music bar called the Doghouse. I was so flustered with my business at the time, I'd actually never noticed him on the building site, so when he asked me out I was a bit surprised. He looked pretty young, six years younger than me, in fact. When he sauntered over to ask me out for coffee I couldn't help being a smartass by saying "Does your momma know you're out, young man?" We both burst out laughing and that was it. As it turned out, we were and still are a perfect match.

We fell in love. Three years later we married and I'm so grateful now because that business, as much as I hated it, brought us together. And I'm grateful to say that after 22 years we are still in love and going strong. Matt has been my biggest support throughout my writing this book. Soon after I met Matt I walked away from the Pie Princess business with nothing to show for three long years of hard work and frustration. Like I said, I wasn't good at business back then and I had no idea how to run one properly. I'd never asked for or gotten good advice from a mentor or anyone who knew what success actually looked like. I just went in with "all the gear and no idea," and as a result, I failed. Miserably.

Even though failure was a bitter pill to swallow, I knew in my gut that success (which was *living life on my own terms*) in business was something I wanted to pursue and win at. I promised myself that next time I'd find a *mentor* before I dove head first into any business venture again. I learnt the hard way, and I never lost the desire to figure out how the *idea* of success was going to become my *reality!*

FRUSTRATED TO FABULOUS
LIFE LESSONS

Okay Gorgeous, it's time to make a nice cuppa (cup of tea). Take yourself and your journal to a quiet area for 15 minutes and write in *detail* your top three-to-five take-away *a-has* from my story so far and from the lessons that follow below.

Be Bold,
Be Courageous,
Be Fabulous!

I learnt many life lessons from starting the Pie Princess business, which I'm sure you'll relate to in your own way. The experience got me thinking about my life and the direction it was heading. For starters, because of my past conditioning as a child, I'd grown up thinking I was going to fail at everything and that I was dumb. It's what I was told at school, and as a child I was always laughed at. I was one of those kids who "just had a go at life." From early childhood I knew I wanted to be successful and have freedom from conformity and money worries. I'd seen enough of that already. Problem was my self-talk was toxic as a result. I was constantly telling myself I wasn't good enough, not smart enough, that I couldn't let people down and I had "no choice." I was spiralling down a deep, dark well, absorbed in self-pity, which was keeping me trapped and small. The relentless and debilitating inner chatter, (which I know you have going on too) was constantly at me, day and night. In fact, did you know that of the 60,000 thoughts we have each day, 95 percent of them are exactly the same as the day before? It's because of our subconscious, because of our patterns of beliefs, thoughts, and habits, which were established in our early years of childhood. And depending on who influenced you the most in your first seven years—your parents, guardians, teachers, authorities, family environment, social environment and friends—your inner belief patterns were set for every area of your life. In simple terms, you model whomever you surround yourself with the most.

When I first heard this (and other facts about our subconscious mind) my first thought was, *Why the hell wasn't I taught about this stuff in school? I've been ripped off!* I was taught to go to school, get a good job, retire at 65 years of age and enjoy a nice retirement, compliments of the government. *What a bloody wrought!* Little wonder I was driving myself nuts! I was living my life according to those same limiting patterns of thoughts, beliefs, habits, and ways of life that I'd learnt as a kid and into my teenage years, a way of life I didn't like or want, thanks very much, doing the same thing day-in, day-out, expecting a different result. Crazy. Up until the age of thirty, before I'd started the Pie Princess mobile food business, I'd already had 33 different jobs. (no, not a typo) and none of them were going to give me the life I had in mind. It was *never* going to happen. That's why I knew I was going to have to find a different way. No matter what it took.

Looking back today, the most important takeaway lesson was that my inner knowing had kicked in, telling me I was born for greater things than who I had become, despite the naysayers and school authorities who insisted on telling me otherwise. I knew I needed to grow and transform myself. My uncontrolled inner-chatter and language was not going to get me far. It certainly didn't match the picture of the person I needed to become in order to get the success I wanted. That much I did know!

I was eager and hungry for answers and I hope you are too. I was open to discovery and possibility because I knew there was more to life than *that!* Besides, millions of people were living the kind of life I had in mind for myself. But how they did it, I didn't know. In fact, at the time I *believed* I didn't know *jack shit!* And I didn't have the skills or confidence to make it happen, at least not yet. But I wasn't about to give up looking for the answers. I knew they were out there, somewhere, and I was determined to seek and find them.

FREE GIFT

www.gdaygorgeous.com/webclass

[3] Video Store

"All success is achieved through the application of power. However, the starting point is a BURNING DESIRE for achievement of a specific, definite objective."

—Napoleon Hill

AFTER THE PIE PRINCESS was laid to rest, I'd learnt my most important lessons, or so I'd thought. My second big opportunity came around from Geoff, my previous landlord, the one who had accepted roast chickens as rental payments when I was short on money. He'd decided to demolish the site where my kitchen had been and build a small shopping centre that included space for a big name-brand video and games rental store. He invited me to

FRUSTRATED TO FABULOUS

become a small percentage shareholder and manage the video store in return. There were three partners in the deal: me, Geoff, and Barry, who was an accountant. My investment to be in the deal was $20,000. Problem was, as usual I was dead broke. The pie van was gone, and I was renting a small apartment that was about falling down near the beach.

Matt and I had become engaged and we'd set the wedding date for April 2000. We saved every dollar we could get our hands on and our budget for the wedding including the reception at Jupiter's Casino on Australia's Gold Coast, was just $4000. Those roast chickens must have really hit a soft spot with Geoff, my previous landlord, because on a "gentleman's handshake" agreement, with nothing formal in writing and no interest owing, he loaned me the $20,000 to pay back when the video shop made profit. As always, Matt was behind me and let me make the decision. It was my life, my journey. I graciously accepted his offer even though my heart wasn't in managing a video store. I don't even know where my heart was, but I used my head, knowing Geoff would be a great mentor for me. He was a smart, wealthy businessman and I have a lot of respect for him. He told me that he gave me the loan because he saw something in me that I didn't see in myself. He said I was a "people person, a marketer," that I was organized and outgoing. Perfect for this role.

That was in *his* mind, at least. In my mind I was *not* confident, and I certainly didn't believe I had the skills to run this business after the *last* episode! The old habitual negative inner-chatter kicked in as usual. *OMG my heart is not in this . . . tell him now! No! Shut up . . . you can't let him down stupid. You owe him BIG time after the Pie*

Princess flop! You HAVE to do this, you don't have a choice! Shit!" On and on it went, for *months* leading up to the grand opening. Geoff had no idea how I was really feeling. I didn't have the guts to say a thing, so I went in fully committed and open to learning all I could. I didn't want to let him down, even though I knew at the moment of agreeing to the terms I was letting myself down.

It wasn't *my* dream, it was his.

Everything was sailing along just fine but after just six months I began to feel like a caged bird in that video shop. I loved my customers, but I did not love managing our video store. I hated it, actually. I began to feel bored and unmotivated. I couldn't see a way out. What was I going to tell my partners? They'd think I was ungrateful and after all, a year hadn't even passed! It felt like Groundhog Day. Being stuck inside all day wasn't my thing. I'd open at 8 a.m. and most days still be there serving customers till closing time at 9 p.m. I felt like the proverbial rat on a wheel. I was missing out on living my kind of life. I was selling myself out. Fear kept me hostage and I suffered in silence like a scaredy cat. I lived a lie and pretended everything was great for another two very, very long years that felt more like ten. In the end I paid the price of fear because I was getting headaches and stomach aches all the time from the stress. But still I kept doing the same thing day in, day out, instead of being honest with myself and my partners and choosing to stand on my own two feet.

I had no idea how fear could play such havoc on my health. The light-hearted, outgoing me was slowly fading away. The lie I was living was eating at me from the inside out. Some of my customers were starting to

FRUSTRATED TO FABULOUS

piss me off! One lady in particular would bring her three kids in to play and run amuck, just so *she* could get a break. *It wasn't a playground for goodness sake, it was a video shop!* I was losing my mind and my temper! I didn't like who I was becoming. All because I was too afraid to say anything, terrified to let my business partners and mentors down. As always, I put other people's feelings before my own, fearing rejection and embarrassment.

Then one morning, a man came strutting in and stood impatiently at the front counter of the video store trying to get my attention. He was a regular customer and usually very happy and chirpy. But not this day. He was pissed off. He'd received a call about a late video that he owed money on, and we'd been chasing him for weeks. He'd come in to see me about it and didn't look the slightest bit impressed. *Oh shit, I* thought, *here we go again.* I heard him out without interrupting once, which was becoming unusual these days. I'm glad I did because he'd been wrongly accused of keeping an overnight video rental for more than three weeks. He had in fact returned it on time. Thankfully he was a nice guy, so he wasn't too harsh on me, just a bit, understandably. After five minutes of conversation, he calmed down, I apologized profusely, and we got into normal chit-chat. I'd learnt a while ago that he was a professional tennis player and coach. He also knew I was very dedicated to my own health and fitness and it was a passion of mine although I didn't get much time to pursue anything outside of the video store. Then he asked me why I continued running a business I clearly didn't enjoy.

God, was it *that* obvious?

Clearly it was. We chatted a while longer and what he said to me next was to be a turning point in my life. He suggested I study and become a personal trainer, because I loved health and fitness and what better way to make a living than having positive impact on people's lives and doing something I loved? I promised him I'd look into it and he was pleased and smiling again as he left the store. I kept my promise, as I always do, and as soon as no one was around, I searched the phone book to see what I could find. (I didn't have a personal computer back then. It was 1999.) I found an amazing personal training college I could attend locally. It seemed like the best choice. I felt my heart race with excitement and possibility. I hadn't felt like that in ages—Maybe this *could* be my ticket to happiness. It was as though I'd received an incredible gift and it was time for me to step up and make some hard decisions. Was I going to continue living other people's dreams or was I going to live my own? I was ready for the latter.

The following week I organized a meeting with my business partners who accepted that I needed to move on. Thankfully one of them agreed to buy my shares.

Thank God!

I paid back the $20,000 loan and walked away from a business, once again. I didn't make much money, but the life lessons were invaluable. I made a promise to myself that from that point on I would *never* spend my days chasing somebody else's goals or dreams. The price to was just too high. Interestingly enough, as soon as I let go of the fear that held me in that business for two and half years, and started being honest with myself and others, my stomach cramps and headaches vanished, almost immediately.

I didn't need a second warning, I got the message loud and clear.

FRUSTRATED TO FABULOUS LIFE LESSONS

Okay Gorgeous, it's time to make a nice cuppa, then take yourself and your journal to a quiet area for 15 minutes and write in *detail* your top three-to-five takeaway *a-has* from my story so far and from the lessons that follow below.

Be Bold.
Be Courageous,
Be Fabulous!

Looking back over this chapter, there were so many lessons, each shaping me into whom I was becoming. I was working hard to shut the inner chatter out, but it was still as strong and loud in my head as ever. The toxic self-talk and the old belief patterns still had a hold on my mind and attitude towards life, but they didn't have a hold on my heart. I had a burning desire for living my life *my way*, but I was nowhere near success just yet. It was going to take a conscious effort to know at a deeper level who I *wanted to become*. Big changes. A true transformation. The gap between where I stood and where I wanted to be was still wide. The same old thinking wasn't going to get me anywhere fast, and I was more *aware* of who I was, what I wanted, and that my old ways of thinking had to go.

Another great lesson was to never go into a business deal with someone just because they have money, finesse, confidence, ability, experience, and you don't. Business partners are like marriages. They take full commitment and unless your values, dreams and goals in life are aligned, it's a big mistake and you'll pay the price in more ways than you bargain for. I was no longer willing to endure the health issues and self-disdain that came from that "opportunity." Would you? *Are you?*

Having said all this, the fabulous part was that I learnt a great deal about managing a business, managing people, negotiating, sales, and marketing from my first mentor. I learnt the value of having someone smarter, wiser, and kind guiding me and teaching me the fundamentals for success, which I am so grateful for and will never forget.

It was time to let go of past regrets, get on with the next adventure and gain some clarity around my real purpose in life. I wasn't getting any younger and life was not slowing down to wait for me. The truth is, even though I'd promised my customer from the video store I'd complete a course to become a personal trainer, I couldn't say right then that it was my life's purpose. I had no clue how to even know what *that* was!

Are *you* relating to any of this? Picture yourself throughout my story and relate the lessons to your own life experiences, anywhere that you can.

What's *your* inner-chatter repeating to you over and over like a broken record? What stories and patterns of self-talk are you mentally running right now? Has society's brainwashing effect kept you small, frightened, or rigid in your beliefs? Do you have clarity around what your true purpose in life is yet? Are your stories holding you back or taking you closer to where you want to get to, and who you want to become in the process? What have you learnt about yourself just from reading these first two chapters?

I hope you're writing as I'm asking these questions. They will get you thinking about your life at a deeper level. Transformation begins with loving yourself and letting go of the past. (More on this later!)

FREE GIFT

www.gdaygorgeous.com/webclass

[4] Get Down and Give Me Twenty!

"Success is neither magical nor mysterious. Success is the natural consequence of consistently applying basic fundamentals."

—Jim Rohn

IMMEDIATELY AFTER SELLING my shares in the video store, I went to college to become a personal trainer. I had to agree with my customer who challenged me, that it sounded like something I'd really like. Thank goodness I followed his advice because it was a major turning point in my life. It was mid-1999 and while studying at college, my mentors introduced me to personal development. It was part of the curriculum and therefore included with every class. We began to learn and understand how to master our mindset as well as the health and fitness side of things. The personal development teachings were based on the "universal laws of nature and attraction" that are globally accepted and incredibly popular today. In fact, many of the masters of the philosophy we studied are globally renowned like the late Earl Nightingale, Napoleon Hill, Jim Rohn, and even Tony Robbins.

I loved these teachings so much I took on extra classes and became a fully qualified life coach at the same time. Sounds weird to me today, saying I was a life coach back then because I certainly didn't feel I had much to offer apart from my upbeat personality and outlook on life. One of the greatest lessons I learnt is that if we work harder on ourselves than in our business, jobs, or careers, we can *become* who we want to be, *do* what we want to do, and *have* what we want to have. In other words, a life by design instead of by default or desperation. After what I'd put myself through previously, working harder on myself than anything else seemed a small price to pay for getting the life I truly wanted.

Before discovering personal development and the "universal laws of nature," I had no clue that it was possible to live a life based on my own goals and dreams. I thought life just happened and we had zero control over how it played out. Discovering the power behind changing my language, being grateful, creating dreams boards, writing down my goals and dreams with some passion behind them, was new, different, and exciting. I mean, who tells you about this stuff growing up? No one in my circle of influence that's for sure! I was hooked, and in all the right ways. I read every personal development book I could get my hands on, listened to all the CDs, watched the DVDs and invested in the mentoring I needed in order to change and transform my mindset. Most importantly, I was implementing and practicing what I learnt daily. I was determined to change my life.

As time went on, I could sense the changes taking place within myself. Sure, I still had and always will have the inner-chatter going on as we all do, but I was now more aware of it, and making an effort to be conscious of what I was saying to myself. Was it making me feel good or bad? That's all I kept asking myself. If I felt good, I knew it was indication I was on the right path. If I felt bad, I quickly did my best to change my thoughts. I learnt that thoughts become things, so I made it my business to spend as much time as possible thinking and writing down all the things I wanted in my life whether or not I had any idea how I'd get them. I'd go for a run on the beach with a Tony Robbins cassette tape playing on my Sony Walkman. I thought he was such a hottie! He had a holiday beach home on the Gold Coast about eight miles from my place at the time, so I'd run up his way in the hopes of seeing him, to let him know I loved his work and how I was changing my life one step at a time. While that dream didn't come true, he was one of the many mentors who had a massive impact on my life, *that's* for certain.

I'd had it with the toxic self-talk. I'd had it with hanging around the *pullers* who didn't want me to change, and I'd had a *gut-full* of doing things I didn't want to do. After a while I noticed that my inner chatter began to change and the negative language I'd use on myself was less abusive. I was learning to let go of past regrets and anger towards others, including my mother, and learning to find ways to be grateful for the experiences that had gotten me to where I was. People were beginning to ask me, "What's happened to you? You've changed. What are you doing?" For the first time in my life I felt intelligent because I passed every exam with flying colours and won many awards from the Institute of Fitness during the following three intense years of self-education. For once I wasn't at the bottom of the class, and it felt good.

I found life had more meaning and I couldn't get the smile off my face.

I love inspiring and helping people, and through a healthier, fitter, body and mind, I knew I could really help my clients transform their lives in different ways once I got my next business started. And in December 2000 with massive excitement and hope for success, I opened the doors to *Royal Personal Training*. I knew in my heart from the work I'd done on myself that I wasn't going to be the average personal trainer. My clients were not only going to get the Royal treatment, they were going to have their lives transformed in ways they'd never thought possible. I had the dream clear in my mind and I couldn't wait to begin. Only problem was I'd opened my little personal training studio with zero clients. I didn't care, I just *believed* I was going to make it this time. Nothing or nobody was going to stop me.

So here was my marketing plan: I'd made friends with lots of people from the video store. I knew many of them had outstanding late fees, so I would call them and ask a favour. Cheeky, but true. I ran this idea past my previous business partners and they were fine with me contacting those clients and offering them my training services to help get my new business off the ground. My idea was to call each customer and ask if they'd come in for *one free* personal training session with me, and give honest feedback based on their experience. So, each afternoon for two weeks I sat in my room, sweating bullets, before I could summon the courage to pick up the phone and call them. I was terrified they'd rejected me or tell me to piss off! Whenever someone answered the phone, I'd quickly blurt out, "Hey gorgeous, it's Amanda from the video store. How are you?" and immediately I could feel the tension through the phone. Clearly, they thought I was chasing them for money. And before anyone had the chance to give me their bull dust story of why they hadn't returned their movies or games on time and shouldn't have to pay the late fees, I launched into my practiced spiel and told them that I wasn't ringing for money, I was ringing for their *help*. Instantly this changed the energy and they were all ears.

I explained how I'd sold my shares in the video store but would really love their help and support by having the one free training session with me in exchange for their honest feedback with no ongoing obligation. Most of them agreed to help me. My marketing plan worked. I had my first thirty *free* personal training sessions booked for my first week in business. Half men and half women aged between thirty and sixty. My perfect demographic.

My attitude about my new business compared to the video store was like chalk and cheese. My personal training business didn't feel like just a business to make money, it was more like *inspired fun* and I truly couldn't wait to support my clients on their journey to better health and happiness. I had my systems in place. My studio was brightly painted and had a great vibe about it and I was ready. The week was fully booked and one by one true to their words, my previous video customers turned up with no idea what to expect. I think some might have been nervous because they knew I wasn't one to dilly-dally around. I was results-driven, and we only had a thirty-minute time slot together. The sessions were short, fairly intense, fun, and energizing. After twenty-five minutes of weight or cardio training, the last five minutes was spent talking about their goals while they enjoyed a nice stretch and a shoulder and neck massage.

After the initial free training session, based on their positive experience I was able to turn those first thirty free sessions into my first twenty-six paying clients. I was ecstatic and many of my new clients were hopeful for the outcomes they wanted to achieve. I offered three different personal training packages:

- 6 weeks,
- 12 weeks inclusive of one free bonus session, or
- 24 weeks inclusive of two free bonus sessions.

On top of this I offered my inspirational life coaching packages, so my clients could enjoy the best results. Most signed up for the twenty-four-week package with the extra two free sessions. A real win for them and me as it insured we had money coming in weekly and more importantly, my clients would get noticeable results. My philosophy was to make each of my clients feel important and worthwhile. We didn't talk about losing inches or getting to a certain weight. Instead, we talked about healthy lifestyle choices, commitment to their outcomes, and having something to look forward to instead of always focusing on what they didn't like about themselves.

One thing I'd do a lot with our ladies is get them to bring in a favourite outfit they wanted to fit back into and hang it on the wall for focus and inspiration. It worked like a charm. Every time they'd whine about how hard I pushed them through their paces, I'd simply point to the outfit they wanted to fit back into and all of a sudden, they'd get a spurt of adrenalin and keep going. We laughed a lot, talked about life a lot, and together with each of my clients, we planned the outcome they wanted to achieve and worked backwards to achieve it.

Word of mouth and referrals helped grow my business quickly and the first year was intense, but I loved every minute of being in that little studio. My clients were getting incredible life-changing results and the atmosphere was always fun and energizing. As I got to know my clients at a deeper level, I learnt so much about people and what they wanted out of life. The biggest surprise was often the way they looked or how much they weighed *wasn't* the most important *or* the only reason for coming to train with me. Through countless, open-hearted conversations, I learnt my female clients were more interested in coming to see *me,* so they could transform their lives and feel empowered, stronger, confident, young at heart and good about themselves. They wanted to feel more attractive, more alive, more love, more connection, more freedom, more successful, and to get more out of life, and of course, to feel less anxious and less stressed with day-to-day life! I totally resonated with the ladies. I was one of them with all the same wants, needs, and desires. I was thankful I'd completed my training as a life coach as the skills I'd learnt really took their lives, my life, *and* my business to a new level of success.

I also organized fun events outside of the training studio, things like beauty treatment workshops with professionals, cheese and wine evenings, and "bring a friend for free" days. My favourite time was when arm-in-arm, over fifty of us completed the 10KM walk during the Gold Coast Marathon all wearing our Royal Personal Training t-shirts proudly. We had a blast and many great friendships were formed. I used to try to set up "blind dates" between my clients. One guy who was an accountant ended up marrying one of the ladies, Anthea. They had a baby girl a couple of years later and that was very cool!

As we grew, I hired three sub-contracted trainers. We were training, coaching, and transforming *one hundred and fifteen* happy clients' lives every week, in my little studio. I loved my work, I loved my clients, and our clients loved us. The business was fantastic *and* financially successful, so what more could I possibly want? For some reason there was something niggling deep in my stomach telling me there was more out there for me, but my mind was stronger now, so I just pushed the nagging feeling down deeper and deeper until one morning I woke up and couldn't get out of bed. My body felt like a massive brick. I was exhausted even though I'd just slept for nine hours. I turned to Matt and said, "I can't do this anymore. I don't want to live my life based on other people's schedules anymore and I know I want more from my life. I have to go find whatever that is." I don't know who was more shocked, me or him.

And just like *that* I'd made up my mind. I think I was trying to catch up to who I'd become from everything I was learning in regard to mastering my own destiny and mindset. The constant niggling inside that I'd pushed down for so long was my indication that if I kept going I'd eventually work out what my *real* purpose in life was. My happiness and well-being were my top values and without hesitation, Matt agreed it was time to go find out what I was made for. I also knew that *he* wasn't that happy with his work either. He was still renovating a property we'd scraped enough deposit to buy. He was working seven days a week to keep it going while holding a fulltime position as a project manager for a big company in Brisbane. Like me, he wasn't yet living his dream life and he had started to complain the past few months. The same morning that I decided to sell Royal Personal Training we went for a long walk on the beach to discuss our decision. Matt wasn't his usual happy self and was whining about how he wasn't happy in his project management role either. It wasn't challenging or fulfilling, and he felt caged in. In my usual soft and calm way, I turned to him and said, "Stop bloody whining and feeling sorry for yourself! If you don't like what you're doing, just change it. Today!"

He couldn't believe my outburst. But I was serious. He'd been complaining a lot lately and I'd heard enough. We talked and walked for more than an hour and by the time we got home he'd decided to resign from the corporate world of building and go find something that was more fulfilling. That afternoon, we spoke with our accountant Ian, who happened to be one of my favourite clients, and after telling him my news, I asked him to help get my business ready for sale. He agreed but needed a month to get my books ready before we could advertise. I instantly felt a wave of relief wash over me. The next month would give me time to think about my next move and get clarity on exactly what I wanted to do with my life.

Royal Personal Training was at its peak. All systems were humming along, from how we answered the phone to how we trained clients, kept data, right down to how each of our clients would get a five-minute shoulder and neck massage with their final stretch at the end of each training session. No matter which trainer our client trained with, the *system* was what the trainers had to follow, and each client had to leave feeling important and worthwhile. They received all the attention they deserved, and it made a massive difference to their lives as well as ours. The business was a well-oiled machine as they say, and it was the perfect time to sell.

Because I wasn't bogged down in the day-to-day, I made the most of that month and each day I'd buy the local newspaper and scour it for ideas as I didn't own a mobile phone or computer back then. Matt had given his notice at work and would be free to find his next adventure in two weeks. Perfect. He could continue his renovating, while I took care of my business and waited for my next big idea to show up. About a week after scouring the papers each day, I came across a small advertisement for a "wealth creation seminar" being held at a local hotel. It caught my eye. It sounded like something I'd like to learn more about, as I'd always wanted to know how wealthy people lived their lives and made their money. We had plenty to learn so I rang, secured the tickets for the following Saturday and told Matt what I'd done. He was interested and agreed that we had nothing to lose and everything to gain. We were excited to see how our next chapter in life was going to unfold.

Saturday arrived, and we got to the seminar early. We were dressed like successful business people even though we weren't feeling so super successful at the time. Dressing for success made us *feel* successful from the inside out. It was about tricking our subconscious minds because the subconscious mind does not know the difference between what is real and what is made up. We wanted to feel confident and successful, even though in our minds we were still far from it. Hopefully this seminar was about to change that.

There were about three hundred people at the event. I couldn't believe how many others wanted to know the secrets of successful people. The energy was electric. I could see the hope and hear the excited voices all around me. Everyone was looking for answers and as frustrated as we were, each waiting in anticipation wanting to find out how they could live a better life. We quickly seated ourselves in the front row. We didn't want to miss a thing! I remember how

I felt that day. Butterflies in my stomach, and the excitement of opportunity and possibility.

The speaker made his way to the stage and everyone went quiet. His name was Adam and he was wearing an expensive chocolate brown suit with matching leather shoes (Italian, probably). From the moment he started speaking I knew that not only was he the real deal, but someday I wanted to be on stage speaking like he was. He was truly uplifting people. He was changing their perception of life and he was giving people hope even if some of them couldn't yet see it. The offer he was presenting was an opportunity to invest to learn how to grow businesses to a high level of success using smart marketing, sales, and sound business principles. Included was a retreat which offered more about the proper mindset and personal development. Not only could we take our lives to another level, we'd learn how to impact other people's lives too. This was the part that really got me excited. I wanted to reach, teach, and impact far more people than I could at the personal training studio.

One small issue. The investment for this training would be $35,000. Both Matt and I looked at each other and felt our hearts sink. I mouthed, "$35,000? *WTF?* as I stared at Matt, both of us wide-eyed. We didn't have that amount of money, but we both wanted in, *badly*. We desperately wanted to change our lives and help others do the same. We wanted our freedom. We wanted life on our terms and it was time to *let go of the past* and make some big decisions.

"Let's find a way," I said to Matt. "We can sell the property you renovated and get a loan, can't we?"

He looked at me seriously and said, "Shit. $35,000? Are you sure?"

"If not now, when?" I said. I was 37 years of age and he was 32. Life wasn't waiting for either of us. We had to make some serious decisions.

Matt continued to look me in the eye and said, "Okay. Let's do it. I'll sell the property and let's go make it work."

And we did. We sold the property, borrowed some money and invested in the opportunity we believed would completely change our lives forever. It was a massive investment for us at the time, but we had no intention of losing it. We were determined to take our lives and our education to another level in order to taste *real* freedom.

Four days after that seminar I was running on the beach when I spotted Adam, the seminar presenter, strolling along enjoying the morning sun. His presentation stirred something much bigger in me than selling marketing packages to small business owners. I wanted to know how to become *like him.* How could *I* be on stage, changing people's lives on a mass scale instead of one-on-one like I'd been doing for nearly three years? *What a buzz it must be for him,* I thought. Not only was he changing people's lives, he was wealthy in most areas of his own life—except of course when it came to his fitness because I could tell from looking at him with no shirt on he could do with some training from me ☺

I plucked up the courage right then and ran straight towards him. He had no option but to see me. I quickly introduced myself and let him know we'd invested into his business opportunity. He congratulated me and politely and asked what I did. With the biggest and best smile I could muster, I told him I was a personal trainer and that *he* could definitely do with a few training sessions as his body resembled a "wet loaf of soft white bread." He looked at me for a moment and we both burst out laughing. Funnily enough he kind of knew I was kidding but at the same time knew he needed the training. My plan had worked. I wanted to train him for free just so I could learn from him. Who knows what could happen from there? We agreed that he'd come to my studio that afternoon and we'd trade training sessions for wealth education. Perfect deal!

I practically flew home to tell Matt and he couldn't believe what I'd said to Adam to get his attention. But who cares, it worked, and I was just being myself.

Adam came to my studio that afternoon, I trained him as hard as he could stand it and we both enjoyed the time together. He was fully committed to his health and never missed a session we had planned. We made an agreement that I'd continue to train him in return for mentoring. It was the perfect deal for both of us. He became strong, lean, fit, and got into peak condition. We trained hard, laughed hard, and worked hard on our businesses and ourselves. And over the coming months Adam, Matt, and I became very good friends. We each had common goals and dreams and we'd talk for hours at a time making plans on how we'd get there. The payoff for Matt and I was just as awesome. Our lives and our businesses went to a whole new level. After investing into the business, we were able to help dozens of struggling personal trainers turn their lives and businesses around.

Soon after, I was invited back to the Fitness Institute (where I'd trained) to become a presenter. I'd share my business, marketing, and sales skills with their students. I loved it, and the students became more inspired as a result. And it wasn't long before we got *far more* than our $35,000 investment back and with the income, Matt secured a couple of little units to renovate. We were feeling good and for once we felt things moving in the right direction for us. Royal Personal Training sold within those two months to another local personal trainer who stepped in and easily picked up the reigns. My clients were sad to see the end of an era, but again, many of them, who I'd grown close to, could see I'd outgrown that phase of my life. They'd all heard me say many times, "I'd rather die knowing than die wondering."

It was time for my next grand adventure and I was open and ready for it!

Matt, about twenty others, and I attended the retreat. It was another massive turning point in my life and cemented the true value of investing in mentors. The "Millionaires' Retreat" turned out to be something completely different than I had imagined. Not only did we dive deeper into marketing and business strategies, the *real* gold was learning to develop our *millionaire mindset* so that we became more consciously aware and focused and could make better choices for what we wanted to achieve in all areas of life. But nothing had prepared me for what I was about to learn. We were mentally challenged beyond anything I'd done before and we learnt that who we had become as a person and everything that we experienced or had going on in our lives, the good, the bad, and the ugly, was *our own fault or doing*.

Ouch!

Our *results* in each area of our life, including our jobs, careers, money, body, spirituality, mindset, relationships, *everything* was our own fault, based on all the choices we had made thus far. My response was, *WTF do you mean, my fault?* It was a hard pill to swallow for every one of us in that room. At first, there was silence, followed by disbelief. *How could my results in life be my fault? Surely there must be a mistake?* I thought. We listened and learnt intently. We were 100 percent focused, open, and interested to find out how this could be. I'd been studying a lot of personal development at the Fitness College and through other avenues, but I'd never heard it in this context before nor had it been explained like this. It was a whole new level of awareness. Both Matt and I were soaking in as much as we could handle. Our lives were never going to be the same again, that was for certain.

Three days later when the Millionaires Retreat came to a close, we both walked away viewing the world around us and the results we had gotten to this point in a whole new light. The gift of what we discovered was worth *far more* than a million dollars. It was time to start sharing the gifts we'd been given with others who wanted to set themselves free of conformity and go make something of themselves and their lives.

FRUSTRATED TO FABULOUS LIFE LESSONS

Okay Gorgeous, it's time to make a nice cuppa, take yourself and your journal to a quiet area for 15 minutes and write in *detail* your top three-to-five take-away *a-has* from my story so far and from the lessons that follow below.

Be Bold.
Be Courageous.
Be Fabulous!

This chapter of my life was to bring many golden lessons. Taking responsibility and ownership for my results being the most valuable for me. Accepting the millions of decisions I'd made stemming from habitual thoughts, feelings, and actions, had landed me exactly where I was and only I could change the course of my life from that point in time, whether or *not* I liked it. With a new view of the world around me, I could see how my childhood and style of upbringing shaped my mind from all that I saw, heard and experienced. It was time to let go of old conditioning by society, outside influences, conformity, school, friends, and family who moulded me to what pleased them. It was evident that keeping the old stories and excuses alive would never bring joy, happiness, fulfillment or success.

The *opposite* in fact.

I'll admit, it's still a work in progress and as you can see, I'm still figuring life out as I go. Thankfully, I've tapped into the guidance of many mentors and still do to this day because I know I wouldn't make it alone. I was so uncomfortable when I got that message. I didn't *want* to take responsibility for all the stuff I'd been through. I felt like I'd been fooled. But there was no escaping the truth. As Michael Jackson's famous song, Man in the Mirror, says, "I'm starting with the man in the mirror. I'm asking him to change his ways." I had no choice but to look inside of myself for the answers I'd been seeking in others and the outside world.

For things to change, first *I* had to change and transform my life, as *you* will. The walls I'd built around myself for protection had to come down. Like an onion when you peel back the layers to get to the sweet stuff inside. I had to stop trying to fit in, stop trying to be someone or something I wasn't. There were amazing lessons from this phase of my life and I was *still* catching up with my awareness of who I was becoming and trying on different "jackets" in the form of different businesses and experiences to see what was right for me. There was *no way* I about to settle for a life that didn't jazz me any longer. Are you? Your life lessons may come in the form of different jobs you have, careers, businesses, relationships, experiences, travel, meeting new people, ideas, books, seminars, friends, online communities—all sorts of wonderful ways. As you move toward your big dreams and goals, it's about giving yourself permission to make these necessary changes because it's impossible to live your burning desires unless you shed your old habits, like a jacket you've outgrown.

Don't look at these lessons as failures. Look at them as growth and as stepping stones that guide you and give you more clarity around what you *do* want. You may need to constantly step out of your comfort zone but remember, as I say, "I'd rather die knowing than wondering."

If you want *your* life to improve in any area, you must first be very clear on your Big Chief Aim, have a Burning Desire to achieve it and know your Big Reason Why (Napoleon Hill). Consciously moving toward your desired outcome or Big Chief Aim is what's important, day by day, experience by experience, lesson by lesson. Don't be afraid. Make a list of all the benefits of moving toward your goals and dreams. Beside it, make a list of what your life will look like in three months, six months, and twelve months if you don't make some bold moves.

How will you feel about yourself if you don't make these new choices, changes, and eventually transformations?

And by the way, your Big Chief Aims and dreams in life won't just happen by chance. It's time *now* to begin your list of what areas of your life need to change, who your mentors will be, and what you can do in this very moment to move one step forward. Make a phone call. Invest in a program, online course, online or offline seminar, online community— discover wherever you need to find your salvation. Invest in yourself. The money, time, and energy will

FRUSTRATED TO FABULOUS

pale by comparison with the value and return you'll experience if you choose your mentors wisely, in *all* areas of your life.

And here's my favourite lesson for this chapter. You're going to pay the price either way, in time or money. It's your choice. But know this. Once time is spent, you'll *never* get it back. Once the money is invested, it will *come back time and time again,* if you invest wisely. Remember, only take the advice or mentorship from someone who has the *results* you are seeking because no one—and I mean *no one else*—is qualified to give it to you.

Listen, learn, act and prosper, girlfriend. It's your birthright.

FREE GIFT

www.gdaygorgeous.com/webclass

[5] The Cat, the Rat, and the Two Dressed in White

"Cherish your vision and your dreams as they are the children of your soul: the blueprints of your ultimate achievements."

—Napoleon Hill

While becoming a millionaire was still on my list of what I wanted to achieve *one day soon*, developing a millionaire mindset was where the *real* riches lay. I realized years before the retreat that money alone wasn't going to make me happy, but it would certainly help my cause and my desire to make a difference in my life and others I wanted to support. And as Napoleon Hill says, "Help other people get what they want, and you'll get what you want." I saw the incredible difference my mum had caused fostering those welfare kids when they lived with us. It had such an impact on my own life that I wanted to have enough money so that once my needs were taken care of, I'd have plenty enough to give to charities and great causes of my choice. Especially I wanted to make sure my parents lived a comfortable retirement for all they'd done for us and others growing up.

My and Matt's minds were being stretched like big rubber bands and we both knew we'd never be or think the same way again after that first Millionaires' Retreat. From there we attended more and more seminars, bought courses, and engaged mentors to help us continue our own transformation in all seven areas of our life:

- Spiritually,
- Mentally,
- Vocationally,
- Financially,
- Family relationships,
- Socially, and
- Physically.

We wanted to be the masters of our own future.

Like I said before, we worked harder on ourselves than anything else and as a result, our confidence grew, our self-belief grew, and a world of possibility opened before our eyes. We were willing to pay the price in time *and* money to grow our minds and reach our goals sooner. Through our one-on-one business coaching for personal trainers and other small start-ups, we were making a difference expanding and growing their minds beyond their own expectations, but *still* we wanted more leverage to reach and empower larger crowds of people. We didn't know exactly how we were going to do that, but we knew something would turn up!

One of our big, chunky goals was to live on the absolute beachfront, as it had been a dream of ours for years. The rents were high and the prices to buy were in the millions. We'd ride our bikes up and down the coast every weekend, looking and daydreaming about a lifestyle that was nowhere near our reality at that time. We'd go to every open home listed by the local real estate agent, just so we could walk through the properties, pretending we could afford to live there. The agents got to know us well and considered us as total time wasters, not that we cared. Then one weekend we went to an open inspection for a ground floor, brand new, absolute beachfront six-story property that had just come onto the rental market. We rang the agent and managed to be the first to view it. The rent was $750.00 a week, which was almost double what we were paying at the time. The value of the apartment was one million, three hundred thousand, and worth every dollar. Soon as we walked in, we both fell in love. We felt like millionaires in more ways than one just standing in the empty living room, although we were *far* from it financially.

FRUSTRATED TO FABULOUS

All we could see was the breathtaking view of the crystal blue Pacific Ocean with gentle waves washing over the white, powdery sand. Families were enjoying the day which was picture perfect. The scene was mesmerizing. It was one of those summer days when there wasn't a breath of wind, nor a cloud in the blue sky. We looked at each other and knew we had to live there. We had a belief that by living in this million-dollar beachfront apartment, we would somehow become successful by default. We'd make it work somehow. We had completed four renovations on other apartments by then and had some savings, which we invested as a deposit into some land in Northern Queensland that was to be developed and built out.

Our deposit was guaranteed to grow into a substantial profit over the following three years. We stupidly believed at the time the profit coming to us from the block of land would well and truly set up our retirement fund and we'd be set for life (but more on that story later). Feeling like we had it all worked out, we signed the rental agreement and moved into the beachfront apartment the following week. Our adored Burmese cat, Mr. Burns or Burnsy Boy, as we liked to call him, took to the beach life instantly and before long became a bit of a celebrity. Burnsy would mosey on down to people sunbaking and kids playing on the beach and hang out with them for hours. He'd roll around in the sand, sit with them and get petted which he loved. He was completely trusting. The lifeguard tower next door was his favourite stomping ground. Everyone knew and loved Burnsy, because he was so outgoing and friendly. If he ever went missing, I'd usually find him upstairs in the bunkrooms of the surf

65

club hanging with the guys. He was an unusually confident cat who had a penchant for adventure.

Another time he went missing for nearly a whole day, which was unusual. He casually sauntered in around dinnertime, as if he owned the place and jumped onto my lap. He smelt awful, like old, musky, mildewy cushions that hadn't seen the light of day or a clean for years. We figured he'd found a new friend somewhere along the beachfront, which had a lot of older houses and had curled up there making himself at home. At least once a week it'd be the same routine—gone missing, come home smelling like old musky mildew. We never worked out whose house he was visiting but that was Burnsy, full of adventure living *his* life like there was no tomorrow.

A few months after we moved in, we had a business meeting organized where a couple were flying in from Adelaide to close a business marketing and mentoring deal we'd been working on for $15,000. They wanted to sit with us in person and get to know us before they signed the check, which we understood, and happily agreed to. Funny thing was, both Matt and I for some reason had white outfits on the day the couple were arriving. We must have looked like total wankers looking back! The couple arrived and when they walked in and saw the view, they looked at each other and the lady said, "I don't care what it costs or what we have to do, I just want your lifestyle!" The husband smiled and agreed with her and it was then that I realized the power of stepping into your dreams and *actually living them,* step-by-step, day-by-day. We didn't pretend to own the apartment, but just being

FRUSTRATED TO FABULOUS

immersed in the atmosphere it created rubbed off on us all.

We got comfortable sitting on my favourite powder-blue suede couches right at the front door overlooking the stunning beach. I had homemade cakes and cups of hot tea for our guests and we were getting along brilliantly. For nearly three hours, we laughed and talked about life, business, current affairs and all sort of things. They felt extremely comfortable with us and our ability to coach and mentor them in their business. We all agreed it was a good fit for them and us and all looked forward to working together. By early afternoon it was time for our guests to leave. As they were about to hand over the $15,000 check for their investment, the lady let out a light scream and pointed towards the door which was ajar letting the warm summer breeze gently flow in. I turned my head towards the door and couldn't believe my eyes. There was Burnsy, pushing his way inside with a big bloodied rat in his mouth. I'd never seen him do that before! Timing couldn't have been worse if he'd tried, the little turd.

The poor rat was half dead and blood was dripping all over the white, tiled floor. The lady and her husband were sitting in shock with no idea what to say or do. I felt the same way. Matt lunged and pushed the sliding doors further open hoping Burnsy would run outside with his catch and disappear. No such luck. He wanted to finish killing the rat and eat it in front of us! The rat wiggled itself out of Burnsy's mouth and tried to limp away. Blood was everywhere, including the bottom of the blue suede couches. Our guests had both feet up, frightened the rat would run towards them in fear.

Burnsy pounced and caught the rat. This time he bit down hard and the rat went limp. He had killed it. I nearly threw up on the spot. Matt was trying his hardest to grab Burnsy and get him outside. We were both so embarrassed.

What a shamble the afternoon was turning into!

Finally, Matt got a hold of Burnsy by his scruff and with the dead rat still in his mouth, almost hurled him through the glass sliding doors, hoping he'd run into the long grass and stay there for a while. But no, he refused to leave and sat directly in our view and proceeded to eat every part of the rat except its tail. I thought to myself, *There goes the bloody business deal. These people surely won't want anything to do with us now!* Matt was scurrying around, wiping up the blood and I was apologizing profusely. Burnsy's timing could not have been any worse.

I turned to our guests who were still sitting, watching the scene unfold with a big grin and simply said, "Well, now you've seen it all. The good, the bad, and the ugly! Welcome to our world." Thankfully they laughed it off and went ahead with the business deal. The lady commented that she felt we were *real, down to earth people* which made her feel more comfortable. And who knows, maybe Burnsy's timing couldn't have been *better?*

After the cat and the rat incident, we had many more fabulous business meetings in our beachfront apartment. It had a sort of magic about it. Whenever people would come over to talk about business or our coaching programs, they'd always be mesmerized by the view and in a way, it helped them elevate their own goals and dreams. We'd talk for many hours, sharing how we visualized every aspect of our lives and how we wanted it to be. We'd talk about the importance of *believing* in yourself and in your goals and dreams, before you *see* the results show up. Slowly but surely our results in life were beginning to transform, as were other people that we had influenced through our coaching and mentoring programs and our income had increased as a direct result of having the courage to *step up* and into our dreams.

We acted like the successful couple we wanted to become, *well* before we actually got there. A bit like successful athletes do, you might say.

We did this in many ways, by dressing, acting, and thinking like successful people do; reading, learning, and educating ourselves like successful people do; even going to beautiful restaurants we couldn't afford, sitting at the bar nursing *one* drink for two hours, because it's all we could afford to do. We'd still ride our bike to all the open beach homes for sale on the weekend, dreaming one day we'd build our own dream home. We'd go and look at beautiful boats and cars just to expand our mind to what was possible, even though we weren't in the market for those things. We tried our hardest to get around more successful people and away from dream stealers. We'd make up dream boards and fill them with pictures of everything we wanted to attract into our lives, even if they seemed unreachable at the time. We learnt the power of writing out in clear detail what our Big Chief Aim in life was and what our Why behind it all was. The *masters* had taught us that if you don't have a crystal-clear and definite chief aim in life, you'll end up aimlessly drifting like 90 percent of the *masses* do.

Drifting through life with no purpose and no aim was *not* our idea of a fulfilling and happy life. We'd often go away on the weekends camping in beautiful Byron Bay on the East Coast of Australia and every morning we'd go to the beach with our journals and write for hours about all the things in life we wanted to see and do. Back then we didn't understand the power of writing out in detail your goals and dreams, but looking back in time now, there isn't a single thing we wrote down that we have not achieved today.

Now, I'm not sharing this with you to brag in any way. My intention is to inspire you to follow and do the same for yourself and your family. Everything is possible if you *first believe* before you *see* the evidence, as I said before.

I remember another time Matt flew to Sydney to go to the annual car show where every dream car that most guys love were on display. The yearly car show in Australia attracts all sorts of weird and wonderful people from all walks of life. This particular time though, instead of wearing his usual shorts, t-shirt and comfy shoes, Matt wore his best suit, just to see what would happen. He wanted to get as close as possible to the latest Maserati that would be on display. As expected, the car he wanted to view was completely roped off, so no-one could get close enough to even touch it. There were two security guards making sure of that! There were people four-deep trying to get a closer look at the car. As he was standing there waiting his turn to view this beautiful car, a salesperson came up to him, put his hand out to shake Matt's, asking if he'd like to step behind the ropes and sit inside the Maserati. The guys standing next to Matt couldn't believe it. Why had he been picked out of the whole crowd? Because he was the only one at the time dressed for success and for whatever reason was chosen to enjoy the experience of sitting in that Maserati. No doubt he made the most of it and sniffed in the brand-new leather smell as much as he could in the few minutes he had.

Matt told me he couldn't believe how awesome that experience was and how by simply wearing a suit that day had made all the difference. He felt successful sitting in that car even though at $300,000 it was *not* in our price range! LOL. It didn't matter. He said just having the opportunity and the experience was the best payoff he could hope for. His confidence and self-belief had taken a boost and that was all that mattered. Those little, yet inexpensive experiences we allowed ourselves to enjoy were the tipping point for us and the fuel that kept us going on our pursuit for freedom and helping others get the same.

Again, we were ready to ramp things up and catch up with our growing identities. Over the next year while living on the beach, we devoted all our spare time to figuring out how to start a business on the Internet. Everyone was talking about it and from what we gathered; the Internet would be our answer to leverage and reaching more people. Again, we invested time and money into more seminars, courses and mentors. In fact, we were so dedicated to finding answers; we flew to Nashville Tennessee to attend our first Internet Marketing seminar. It was 2003 and there was a whole world to discover online.

It is our belief and experience that if you surround yourself with people who have the results you want, you'll learn to think and act as they do. Model them, as Tony Robbins says. Our eyes and minds were opened up to a world we knew practically *nothing* about. The speakers shared their own stories of how they began and went on to incredible success. The seminar went for three full days and there were more than one thousand attendees. Because we invested in two of the programs when offered, we got to hang out with the speakers and ask them questions. We wanted to know their stories. How did they start and what possibilities did the Internet bring? In one of the last sessions on the third day, all of the twelve speakers were lined up on stage for an open question panel. Dozens of people waited their turn. When they'd gotten through them all, Matt put his hand up and was handed the microphone to ask his question. But he didn't ask a question about internet marketing. He stood up and addressed the whole panel of twelve speakers and asked one question.

"How do I get to be one of you up there?"

My cheeks flushed from embarrassment. We didn't even own a website for God's sake! How could we be a presenter? I kept my eyes on the panel of speakers anxiously waiting their response. You could hear a few sniggles from the crowd and one of the women speakers had a smirk on her face. Five of the twelve speakers responded to the question, although you could see what they were thinking by the surprised look on their faces. They were all polite and agreed that to be on stage you had to have *proven results* in the field you wanted to present on. You needed to be able to show other people how to get those same results, in a systematic way so they too would have success if they followed as described.

Finally, the woman speaker took the microphone, looked at Matt with a big fake smile and said, "It'll be unlikely you'll get to be on this stage. You're too new with no experience on the Internet. Best to keep going for a few years and see what happens."

Matt smiled at her and with a slight laugh said, "Watch this spot. I'll be on that stage one day. Thanks for your encouragement."

With that he sat down and stared forward the rest of the question period, not saying a word. I couldn't *believe* what she'd said to him. I knew my face was red but not from embarrassment this time, from frustration at how she tried to make a fool of him. It was *totally* uncalled for. Matt patted my leg and looked at me. In that very moment I knew in my heart this woman had in fact ignited something in him and his look said to me that her comment would drive him to the success he desired.

After the event closed we headed to the bar. I was ready for a bubbles and wanted talk about what we'd learnt over the three days and also what had just happened. Matt grabbed my hand and squeezed it while we walked and said, "Honey that was the best thing that ever happened to me! Her comment will drive me until we become successful and can help other people live their dreams too. You watch!" Well, he didn't need to convince me, I knew he meant what he said, but the truth was, *we were* new to the internet world and didn't even have a website! How were we going to be successful enough to be on stage helping other people? I let it go and for the rest of the night we hung out laughing and chatting about our experience with other people we'd met over the three days.

The next morning, we headed to the airport to fly back to Australia with a world of possibility in front of us. Matt was hooked on the idea of making money on the Internet and then one day, after creating success for ourselves, showing other people how to do the same. I wasn't so convinced. I was a more a tactile type of person. I loved being with people. How was I going to get fulfillment from the Internet? Problem was, I couldn't deny what I'd seen and heard at the Internet seminar. If we were looking for the leverage we wanted in time, money, and helping others, the Internet was the only way to go.

Even though I loved working with personal trainers, small start-ups and teaching at the Institute of Fitness where I'd trained, I was open to discovery. I knew I had more in me and Matt was on a mission! We were both trying to catch up with our own mental growth and who we'd each become, and Matt was *certain* the Internet held the answers. I didn't know what was possible, but I believed something would show up and we'd find out soon enough.

FRUSTRATED TO FABULOUS LIFE LESSONS

Okay Gorgeous, it's time to make a nice cuppa, take yourself and your journal to a quiet area for 15 minutes and write in *detail* your top three-to-five take-away *a-has* from my story so far and from the lessons that follow below.

Be Bold.
Be Courageous,
Be Fabulous!

This chapter of my life brought such a myriad of life lessons I barely know where to begin! In various ways as I unravel my story, I know you'll be relating with me and seeing yourself in similar situations. The frustrations, wins, losses, emotions, and the rollercoaster of life. I discovered a long time ago that we are born to continually grow and expand as humans through life's experiences, whether they're painful or inspirational. My view is that I'd prefer to grow, expand, and experience my life fulfilling my dreams rather than live with painful regret.

Wouldn't you?

The sad truth is most people wander aimlessly through life hoping, wishing, and praying for better outcomes. Worse still, they have no clear goals because they don't believe in themselves or their ability to *be, do or have, anything* they set their hearts and minds on. Health, wealth, and happiness elude them and because they don't understand why, they join the mass mentality and sometimes grow to despise others who seem to have it all.

Know anyone like this or had the experience yourself?

I'll admit girlfriend, I've been guilty of *all* the above!

Tony Robbins says, "The masters believe before they see, the masses must see before they believe." The question is; which category do *you* fall into?

For years I was definitely in the "masses" category. I didn't know how to think for myself because I was a follower of other people's dreams. I tried to fit in, but in the end, I was miserable trying. Until I stumbled across these teachings beginning in 1997, I was like most other people wandering through life accepting jobs, relationships, and business opportunities I knew in my gut weren't right for me. But reading my story you know the fear of criticism, failure, and not being liked or accepted was far greater than my desire to focus on what *I* wanted from life. I wasted years and years, stuck in a cul-de-sac trying to fight my way out of society's conformity and what others expected of me.

My true hope is that *you* won't do the same.

Problem is, most people don't even know *what* they want, *why* they want it, and have never bothered to thoughtfully write out their goals and dreams, let alone take the right and necessary action to achieve them. In fact, most are too scared to even *think* about them because fear holds them back. Usually it's the fear of *criticism* from others. *Next* comes the fear of failure. Imagine being Matt when he asked the speakers how he could be on stage like they were. The sneers and

FRUSTRATED TO FABULOUS

giggles—and not even behind his back! We could hear and see them. But he stood his ground, and so must you.

Yet unless you are crystal clear on the areas of your life you want to transform and have a burning desire for results based on your big reasons why, you will never accomplish them because your old habits and ways of thinking will sabotage you and pull you back to where you're at.

Every single time.

I know that Matt and I would have packed it in dozens of times if it weren't for our "big reasons why" list. We hand wrote it out, tweaked it constantly, and read it aloud every day until in our hearts we *actually believed* those goals and dreams would come true long before they did. It's worth saying again—your subconscious mind (the one that holds you hostage with your old ways and conditioning) does not know the difference between truth and lies. This is why if you tell yourself a lie *over and over* again, soon enough you'll believe it to be true.

We've all done this right?

I know I have!

Girlfriend, I cannot emphasize how important your "big reasons why" list is. I don't know what areas of your life you want to transform, maybe a few? Either way, begin writing your list today. For example, if you're worried about your health and you're carrying excess weight, your "big reasons why" list could be based around wanting to move with ease, wanting to play with your kids easily without pain, wanting to get off the medication you know is doing more harm than good, wanting to fit into last summers' dress you love, and to feel fabulous, full of vitality, wanting to live a longer, happier healthier life, perhaps. You can choose more than one area of your life. We had at least one hundred items on our first "big reasons why" list. Slowly but surely, step-by-step, day-by-day changes began to happen and then over time, a *true life-changing transformation.*

And another tip: It's *important* to understand that *change and transformation* are quite different:

- *Change* occurs when you modify your actions and behaviours in the short term.
- *Transformation* occurs when over a *period of time* you no longer *want* or *desire* to go back to old habits and old ways of life.

It's just like a cocoon that truly does transform over a period of time into a beautiful butterfly.

It is for this reason that you *must stay consciously aware,* guarding your *thoughts, feelings, and actions* if you want to transform, grow your wings, and live a life you love. Your own mind will be your biggest obstacle, no matter what your current situation is. You only need to look at your current lifestyle and results to know where you are right now. The great news is, if you are willing to work *harder* on yourself than *anything* else, like we did, and learn these universal, timeless laws, you will truly transform like a beautiful butterfly.

FREE GIFT

www.gdaygorgeous.com/webclass

[6] G'Day L.A.!

"Your outer world of attitudes, wealth, work, relationships and health will always be a reflection of your inner attitudes of mind."

—Brian Tracy

Arriving home from Nashville, Tennessee we made a decision to wind down the coaching business for personal trainers and other small business owners and my lecturing at the Institute of Fitness, till we decided our next move. Great thing was that we could easily pick up where we'd left off with this particular business model anytime we chose to. But once we'd had a glimpse into the "internet" world, Matt was hell-bent on finding a way to leverage our time and resources via the World

Wide Web. He was studying and had completed a variety of different courses while I thought about how I was going to make this transition. I was open to it, but I wasn't grasping it as easily as Matt was. We were tossing around a variety of ideas from downloadable e-books, to online courses—all sorts of crazy, interesting ideas. Then one day, a few weeks later, our best friend, *out of the blue*, suggested we co-create romantic audio books for couples, who wanted more meaningful and deeper relationships. As far as we knew there was nothing on the market like it that was classy and attractive for everyday couples.

We all loved the idea, and not only would it meet our needs for a more leveraged business and lifestyle, but more importantly we'd be enhancing couples' lives all over the world. Because the three of us had been best friends for a while, we knew each other's strengths and weaknesses and thought it would be something really cool to create together. We agreed to have the audio books written and recorded by professional writers and actors in Hollywood because the product was being produced for the American market and we wanted our products to be world class. We had absolutely *no* experience in this field and conducted *zero* market research, however our excitement and our self-belief were driving us forward at a rapid pace. Within two weeks of making our decision, we'd hired our professional storywriter and our actors through a Hollywood agency we'd found online. The three of us were pleased with ourselves and what we'd accomplished and were imagining couples all over the world blissfully listening to the high quality, classy, romantic audio stories we produced.

FRUSTRATED TO FABULOUS

We were still living in Australia on the Gold Coast and most mornings we'd go to the gym, train together (I was still cracking the whip, "Get down and give me twenty!") and we'd always then hang out for two or three cups of tea afterwards. One morning as we talked excitedly about our new business adventure which was almost four weeks old, our friend made a *joke* that we should all pack our bags and move to Los Angeles, so we could make connections, get a better feel for our market and really focus on the business. For a moment there was silence as we all digested what had just been said. Matt knew that America was on my bucket list of places to visit again, but never had I thought about *living* there. Matt's eyebrow was slightly raised, indicating the suggestion wasn't off the table. My heart rate went up as I turned to my friend and asked if he was serious.

"Yep, why not?" he said. "If we're gonna do this, let's do it right. We've only got one shot at it and if you two are up for the adventure, I'm in, boots and all." You could have knocked me off my chair with a feather. He was *dead-set-serious all right*.

I looked back at Matt and without a word of a lie, in unison we said, "Stuff it, let's go for it. We're in boots and all, too." The decision was made just like that and laughing at the thought of how spontaneous and crazy the idea was, we all knew our lives would never be the same again. None of us were time wasters and we all made decisions quickly if there was enough information and it made sense at the time. We talked and planned our adventure for another three hours over more cups of tea and toast. By the time we left we were all convinced that if we couldn't make our business work in America, we'd never make it work at all. We planned to leave for L.A. in exactly six weeks for six months of business and adventure, and after that, we'd find a way to work things out. None of us were able to stay any longer because of visas, but who cared? We'd figure *something* out!

We left the café, went home, and began the arrangements to pack up our lives and move to L.A. I raced to the phone and rang Mum to tell her our news and all she said—*God love her,* was, "I'm not surprised Amanda, you're always doing something crazy chasing your dreams. Good for you! Go do what you want to do. I can't wait to tell your father when he gets home!" Nothing had changed. She always let me make my own decisions without giving me too much guidance. I used to be angry with her for that, but I was beginning to *love* her for it. We happily, but sadly (for leaving the home we loved) packed up the beautiful beachfront apartment which held such happy memories and moved into a tiny apartment owned by a friend of Mum and Dad's for the last six weeks so we could save every dollar possible. Burnsy the cat was moving in with some of our longest and dearest friends, Megsy and Kenny. Megsy was delighted because she and Burnsy had quite a special bond since he'd been a kitten. Kenny had no choice, so he went along with what Megsy wanted.

Our life's belongings had to fit into three suitcases between us. And *shit, that* wasn't easy! I had so many pairs of shoes girlfriend, it was *so* hard choosing which to take or leave. Matt didn't understand my dilemma so I shoved as many pairs into my two suitcases as possible, allowing him the third suitcase for his own stuff. Talk about stressful!

Those final six weeks flew by. There was so much to do. Moving across the planet was no small feat, especially trying to launch a new business. We still needed to sell our car, store furniture and belongings, and sever ongoing financial commitments we no longer needed. We had to organize bank accounts, tie up loose ends from previous business dealings, find accommodations in L.A, and throw farewell parties. The list was long! All our friends were laughing at us and could not believe what we were about to embark on, but secretly I could see some were envious that we had the guts to go chase our dreams and be happy. We told everyone we were going to make it in America, the land of opportunity, and *they'd see!*

Finally, the day rolled around and the big black car taking the three of us to the airport in Brisbane pulled up outside the unit we were staying in. Mum and Dad came to see us off and as we headed towards the highway on our way to *the land of opportunity called America,* I remember thinking to myself, *What the heck have we just done this time?* I pushed the thought away and joined in the boys' excited conversation. We were off on an exhilarating adventure full of possibility and nothing was going to put a damper on it. We arrived at the airport, checked in, and waited in the lounge feeling overwhelmed with excitement, dreaming of what would become of us. We must have looked and sounded like three happy clowns laughing, joking, and making up stories of how we were going to be rich and famous within a couple of years. Truth is, *we actually believed it!*

AMANDA JANE CLARKSON

We landed safely and for the first two weeks till we moved into our permanent accommodation in Marina Del Rey, we decided to stay in a hostel in downtown Hollywood. *Bloody hell,* talk about a rude awakening of how a big city like Hollywood works! It was the middle of June and it was hot but not muggy like our tropical summers on the Gold Coast of Australia. The energy was electric, and the streets crowded with hustlers and holidaymakers. Everyone seemed to want to be rich and famous and Hollywood was where they came in droves to make their dreams come true. Nobody cared who you were, what you looked like, or where you'd come from. I fell in love with L.A. *on the spot.* The people, atmosphere, energy, excitement, and opportunity abound, and I couldn't get enough of the place. Even the crazy traffic didn't bother me. I was where I wanted to be and all I could see was a thriving, bustling city where dreams overflowed, and people could be their authentic selves.

Even though we were on a tight budget, we made the most of every minute and just around the corner from the hostel was the small recording studio where our hired actors and actresses would go to record our romantic audio books for couples each day. None of us had ever experienced working with actors and actresses before. They were a different breed to us Aussies, but jeez they were *brilliant* at their craft. Each day we'd arrive at 11 a.m. and watch our two talented producers create magic with the end result being very a classy product. During the day we worked hard on our new business. Matt was in charge of preparing the internet marketing side of things while our mate handled the creative side of things and I worked with our writer to make sure the stories were *exactly* what we wanted. It was an experience I'll remember for the rest of my life. It was June 2004 and living in L.A. was a dream come true for me, although Matt missed the beach life and especially his daily surf routine. The water was cold in L.A. compared to Australia but the small sacrifices we made to live our dreams was so worth it.

After two weeks living in Hollywood, it was time to move to Marina Del Rey and settle into "normal" life, whatever *that* looked like. I took to living in L.A. like a duck to water, and while the boys were excited about the business side of things, they weren't as keen as I was to try and extend our stay past the six months we had, but we agreed to live like the locals while we were there and enjoy every moment of it. And we did. We made friends easily. I find Americans super-friendly and if in any way they could help you, they would. *God bless America!* We spent every weekend visiting people, exploring new, exciting cities and beaches, and spending time getting to know the locals around Venice Beach. It was a time in my life when I felt free, adventurous, and open to what could be. Again, through this experience, our minds had expanded to another level and I'd say it was one of the best choices I had made in my whole life.

Three months after arriving, production wrapped up and it was time to go to market. Matt had a professional website built and used all his new skills to do his best at marketing. Being new to the Internet, none of us were masters at this game and to be honest the day we launched our website we'd hoped for hundreds of sales.

Talk about all the gear and no idea!

Still, we didn't give up hope. We kept at it until two months in. The money was running out and the bills were piling up. When we began this adventure all the money we had except for the deposit we'd put on the land in North Queensland (which I'll get to soon enough) was fifty thousand dollars left to our name. By the end of the second month living in Marina Del Ray, our savings had dwindled to the last few thousand dollars and we still needed money to continue marketing a product that no-one was buying. Things were looking bleak. We'd bought a car and had settled into local living nicely, but time and money were running out, and because we didn't have a working visa, we needed to make some big decisions and *fast*. By the time the fifth month rolled around, our best friend said he wanted to come home to Australia. It wasn't working out and really none of us had the money or visas to stay past the next month. Matt agreed, but *I* wanted to stay. I was so desperate to stay I even thought about setting up an Aussie "sausage sizzle" pop-up stand on the famous Strip in Venice Beach, but Matt wouldn't hear of my schemes. It was time to face the reality of our money and visa situation and come home before we had zero money left. I was gutted, but this time I had to agree, we had no choice. By law, we couldn't stay past the next month anyway. By then we'd made a few friends and let them know our circumstances. I could see they were disappointed for us but no doubt they'd seen dozens of people like us rock up to America with stars in their eyes looking for fortune and fame.

We said our goodbyes and gave away all the stuff we'd bought to set up home over the past five months—bikes, clothing, furniture, food, books—all the things we couldn't drag back to Australia. We each packed our suitcases and arranged to come home with heavy hearts and a story we didn't want to tell because we were so embarrassed that we had failed. Months before, we'd believed we had found the "one" that was going to be our ticket to freedom while impacting people's relationships in magical ways. It wasn't to be. We arrived home feeling dejected and like absolute losers. We'd failed big time in a country with a population of more than three hundred million people. How embarrassing! We could see the looks on their faces of the people back home and the comments from some of them already—*'I told you so!'* and *'Well, at least you can always go back to what you were doing before mate.'*

Yeah, right, *not!*

And because we had nowhere to live and practically all of our money was gone, we literally didn't know what to do or who to turn to. We had no choice but to ask Mum and Dad for help. Mum was managing four 8-room motels along the Gold Coast Highway and one of the motels was called The Red Emu. It was neat but tired looking, painted white with maroon trimming. It was situated directly across the road from the Crown Casino and often would attract a certain type of clientele that would drive in and rent the rooms by the hour. (You get my drift, right?) Mum was awesome at her managing role and made anyone and everyone feel at home. She had a real talent for her role and made friends easily with people from all walks of life, never judging them and always accepting them with a smile. She knew we were homeless, embarrassed, and needed a hand up for a couple of weeks till we got ourselves sorted. Kindly, she offered for us to stay in one of those rooms for two weeks at her expense until we worked our life out. As much as we balked at the idea of staying in that motel, we were very grateful and accepted her offer. I remember pulling up in a cab and checking in. It was a Friday afternoon and the No Vacancy sign was lit which meant there'd be plenty of weekend action at the Red Emu Motel!

Great.

Mum was there, and she was all smiles and laughter trying to make the best of an awkward situation. Matt was in no mood for laughter but was thankful she wasn't giving us a hard time about what we'd just gone through. That was another thing about Mum, she didn't ask too many questions or get too involved in my life, which sometimes used to piss me off but on this occasion, I couldn't have been happier about. We headed towards room 3 and pushed open the brown door that could've done with a new lick of paint. The room was clean and tidy with one double bed, a small, under-counter brown bar fridge. There were coffee and tea facilities and a tiny bathroom with a small shower and toilet. Not exactly the beachfront apartment we'd given up almost eight months prior, but who were we to complain? It was more than some people had, so we shut up and forced a smile as a lump rose in my throat and tears blurred my vision.

Mum quickly left us alone to settle in and as Matt slumped onto the saggy bed that had seen too much action in the past, he looked at me with pain in his green eyes and said, "How the hell did we end up here, living in the Red Emu Motel?" I felt sorry for him, and sorry for myself as the tears rolled down my face. I sobbed quietly so Mum couldn't hear. The walls were thin, and I could see her hovering outside in case we needed anything. For once in my life I couldn't try to blame anyone. We'd taken the risk and this time for dozens of reasons the odds weren't in our favour. We agreed we'd stay under the radar for a while and not tell our friends or other family members we'd failed and had to come home. And worse, come home with no business and most of our savings gone.

Our friend was in the same boat and quietly slipped off to live with another mate of ours, till he got back on his feet. We all needed time out to think about what we would do now. After selling our few belongings or giving them away in L.A. we arrived back in Australia with less than two thousand dollars. This grand adventure had set us back almost *forty eight thousand dollars*. We'd have to start again. I was forty-one years of age and wondered if I'd *ever* figure business and life out. Matt was thirty-five. With no plan and battered egos we held on to the belief that somehow we'd find our way again.

Frustrated to Fabulous
Life Lessons

Okay Gorgeous, it's time to make a nice cuppa, take yourself and your journal to a quiet area for 15 minutes and write in *detail* your top three-to-five take-away *a-has* from my story so far and from the lessons that follow below.

Be Bold. Be Courageous. Be Fabulous!

This time in my life brought some hard but necessary lessons I'm certain you'll relate to in dozens of ways. We'd acted on impulse before even knowing if there was a market for our products and paid the price of naivety. Having said this, outside of business, my spirit of adventure and being open to possibility beyond my comfort zone was alive and well. This is a major lesson I'd like you to consider.

You are an incredible creator and if you're not living your most amazing, authentic life in all areas, then you must *stop, think and be honest* with yourself. What *exactly* is holding you back? Are you open and willing to step out of your comfort zone and see what this incredible life has on offer? Or are you allowing fear to sabotage your goals and dreams like most of us do? Don't worry, you're not alone if you admit that you do, because the great news is, you can begin to make small changes day-by-day, step-by-step, until the "new you" emerges and your goals and dreams start to become your reality. But it begins with awareness of where you're at now and a clear vision of where you want to be.

Learning from my experience and story, you'll notice a pattern of how by working harder on our mindset and attitude than we did anything else, we

FRUSTRATED TO FABULOUS

were able to continually pick ourselves up and keep moving towards our dreams even in times of adversity. Looking back over your own life, if you can relate to these stories, make notes of how you handled similar situations. What were your feelings, self-talk, out-ward talk, and actions? Can you see that the more you put yourself "out there" and actually go for your dreams, the more possible it is that you will fail many times? Great thing about failing or "falling forward" as Matt likes to say, is that it's just another lesson to learn and if you accept that falling down and having to pick yourself back up is a crucial part of growth, while shedding your old habits and beliefs, I promise you will reach your goals and dreams.

Fear is what's going to stop you. That's it. And this is exactly why you must always carry with you, your written Chief Aim or Major Goals and Dreams, and your Big Reasons Why list in a condensed version, so that when you're facing times of adversity you can read it and the desire for your goals and dreams will keep you going.

And that advice is gold—please underline it now!

I actually have a condensed version of mine that I keep under my clear phone case cover, so that it's visible anytime I need a "nice cup of concrete, or a pick me up." ☺

Question: When was the last time you stepped out of your comfort zone to go after your dreams with everything you've got? Have you ever packed your bags and moved to another town, city or country? Have you resigned from a job or career because you know it's eating you from the inside out, if it's not right for you?

Have you ever plucked up the courage, sat down and carefully planned with meticulous detail your "perfect day" and "perfect life" just as you would if you were going on your dream vacation or building your dream home? These are the lessons worth sitting and pondering on, wouldn't you agree? When was the last time you actually woke up, felt immense gratitude for your life, and got out of bed with a smile knowing you were heading into a well-thought-out, exciting day that was taking you closer to your dreams, whatever they are for you?

If you can't remember the last time you felt *that* good in the morning don't worry, you're not alone and it's not your fault. Most people have never been taught to think about or even plan their lives. They believe life just happens. But girlfriend, I'm here to share with you that you *can* choose how you live your life, if you have a big enough desire to do so.

Life is short wouldn't you agree? So *if not now, when?*

You don't need or want to live with fear, envy, jealousy, anger, frustration, or regret. The good news is that if you feel any of these emotions, you *can* change and transform into the woman you long to be. Become the "new you," beginning today. Take your time absorbing these lessons I'm sharing with you. I believe at some level you'll see yourself in many of the situations I've been in and experienced but in your own unique way and through your own unique experiences.

How do you want your life to play out?

If you haven't already done so, now is the time to plan the rest of your life in as much detail, including dates and times, as you can. Begin where you are, it's never too late and remember, for your dreams to come true in the area of life you want to pursue, you *must* include your Big Reasons Why list because this is the *real* magic that'll get you there. If planning your whole life feels like too much in one go, start with just one area and one dream at a time. Write down the goal and dream. Then in detail describe in writing *what* you want and *why* you want it. The more detailed, the more likely it will become believable to you. Make sure you feel it with as much as you can. It will then become your reality if you take the required action. Even if you have no idea *how* your dreams will become your reality, write them down anyway because if your WHY is big enough, the HOW will come to you in due course.

For your own sake, please don't' take what I'm sharing here lightly. In my wildest dreams I had no idea how our dreams would come true, but they did because the more I prepared myself and got clear, the more opportunity showed up.

Begin today. Let's see where the magic can and will take your life.

FREE GIFT

www.gdaygorgeous.com/webclass

[7] Careful What You Wish For

"Ask and it is given."

—Abraham Hicks

MOVING BACK TO AUSTRALIA after our experience in L.A. had certainly taken a toll on my confidence. Embarrassed and disappointed in myself for the mess we'd created and gotten ourselves into, the old feelings of how I felt at school when I failed almost *every* subject, came flooding back to haunt me. The memories of being laughed at, taunted, and being told I was dumb and wouldn't amount to much made me wince. It was the reason I left school at the end of grade ten, at just sixteen years of age. *How the hell* were we going to face our friends and the rest of the family who we hadn't even contacted yet because we were too humiliated and weren't up for the hundreds of questions we knew they'd fire at us? No doubt, some would have genuine sympathy, and others would be secretly pleased with our unfortunate news. I began to question my ability as to whether or not I had it in me to keep going for my goals and dreams. The old destructive inner chatter was at it again—

Who do you think you are?

You're not smart enough to run a business! Stick to a job, it's safer!

I told you so, dumb ass! What were you thinking?

Now look what you've gone and done. How're you going to explain this one away? How embarrassing!

Everyone's gonna think you're an idiot! Why couldn't you make it work? You were out of your league, that's why, dipstick!

Stop trying to be someone you're not and just be normal like everyone you know for once, will you?

On and on and on it went, poisonous self-talk that wouldn't let up. I could feel myself slipping into a state of hopelessness and I knew if I didn't get a handle on it, I might slip deeper into a place I didn't want to go. Although Matt was going through the same experience, he seemed to be handling the situation much better. He wasn't anywhere near as miserable as I was because he was home back near the beach where he could surf and find peace within. He was confident we'd get out of the mess we'd created. I was holding my emotions in check but the panic was there, no doubt about it.

Were we ever going to make it? I asked myself that question dozens of times a day. *Probably not, idiot,* the toxic inner-voice would answer back. *Stuff you,* I'd say to myself. My heart ached to be back in L.A. where I felt I belonged, but that wasn't going to happen, no matter how hard I clutched to the past. It was time to face the truth and make some tough decisions. We'd been living and hiding at the tired, old Red Emu Motel for three long, miserable weeks. With no plans and nothing to do all day, we had plenty of time to reflect and talk about what had gone wrong and how we could have done things differently. With confidence at an all-time low, we plugged into our mindset mentors through audios and videos, spending hours a day listening and writing our new set of goals and dreams. We learnt from one of our mentors that we needed to stop wallowing in the past, be grateful for what we had now, and get excited about a new future.

That was the key that opened our hearts and minds to new possibility.

Thank God for the mindset mentoring. It truly got us back on our feet and I know in my heart things would have turned out much worse if not for the daily coaching and inspiration. We were already wealthy in so many fabulous ways. We just had to stop feeling sorry for ourselves and look at things in a new light. We had our health, each other, family who loved us, and great friends. We lived in a beautiful city, we breathed clean air, walked on stunning beaches. Our sky was mostly blue because of where we lived. We drank clean water. We were rich with knowledge, ideas,

FRUSTRATED TO FABULOUS

and options. The list was long. In fact, we wrote down more than *three hundred* things to be grateful for in this life! We had absolutely nothing to complain about. It was just *how* we were viewing life that made all the difference.

The grieving stage was over, it was time for a nice big cup of *concrete* and to get on with life. We made a pact not to keep going over what was or could have been. There was no point and it certainly wasn't going to help us move forward. We were hanging onto the fact that we still had the block of land in Northern Queensland, believing it would be our nest egg one day. There was far more to be thankful for than we were seeing, and it was time to turn a new page. With our remaining savings we rented an apartment overlooking the beach. The stunning city of the Gold Coast where we live has beaches that stretch for almost thirty-three miles (or just over fifty-two kilometres). Seeing the beautiful, crystal-clear, blue Pacific ocean and white powdery beach brought so many happy memories back we felt instantly charged and ready for new beginnings.

Burnsy our Burmese cat was back home with us and seeing him after more than six months was the highlight for us. Megsy and Kenny had spoilt him rotten as usual and were sad to see him leave but it was time he came home. We'd missed his antics plus he was extra cuddly and needy which suited me fine. He was my little guy.

We organized a barbeque for our friends and family so we could get the questions over and done with. We'd kept very low-key till this point, as we wanted to avoid as many "I told you so" comments from well-meaning family and friends who couldn't wait to hear the details of how we'd made fools of ourselves. It was interesting, watching and hearing the responses as slowly we opened up about our time in L.A. and how the three of us had hustled for almost five months before we literally had to come home because of visa and money issues. Even though at an unconscious level a few of our friends were rather pleased we'd failed as it made them feel better about their shitty lives, there were others who were truly humbled by our stories. They loved the spirit we had for not living with conformity and what society says we should or shouldn't do—to be like the masses, take limited risks, plan for mediocrity, and hope for the best.

I could tell by the looks on their faces and encouragement they wished *they'd* had the courage and strength to go after their own dreams and goals. They were fascinated with our stories and wanted all the gripping details of the good, the bad and the ugly experiences. No doubt, in some way they were imagining what their lives could have been, *if only...*

We got to the end of the day and after we'd answered the questions, laughed at life and shared some hilarious stories, we were feeling more like our old selves, more hopeful and curious about our future. Matt still held strong to the belief that the Internet held our answers. He kept saying to me, "All I want is a home-based internet business that makes $2,000 a week working part-time, and to have no financial stress. I know it's out there somewhere"

It was February 2005 and I was still working out what I'd do next with my life. Matt was still trying to crack the Internet and by now the money was getting low. There was no way I was getting a job—I just *knew* something would turn up. It always did. Then a week or so later Matt got an email about making money on eBay and flicked it to me because he thought I might find it interesting.

Interesting? Shit, not only was it interesting to me, it actually made sense! Now you've got to remember it's 2005 and eBay was incredibly popular, and Amazon would not arrive in Australia for another decade at least. From what I could tell from the email, eBay had the customers, credibility, and opportunity for anyone, no matter their age or background, to set up a business and run it from anywhere in the world. I recall my heart was racing and in that instant I knew eBay was the answer I'd been looking for as far as the Internet and leverage of time and money went. I could grasp the concept. It was visual and easy to navigate, with thousands of categories we could grow a business in. The email had a link which led to a web page offering a home study course written by an eBay millionaire for the investment of US$3,000. I wanted the course because I knew to be successful I'd need a mentor. Problem was, we didn't have US$3,000. We barely had the rent money.

By some stroke of incredible luck, the very next week we were offered a credit card from our bank to the value of AU$50,000!

Can you believe it? At first, I couldn't! Why was a bank offering such a high amount of credit to us? We were almost broke, for God's sake. But not being one to look a gift horse in the mouth as they say, we signed and accepted the credit card. We were back in business

AMANDA JANE CLARKSON

even though it was just a loan, *but who cared?* We invested in the course and every day without fail, I'd diligently go through and complete every lesson and do exactly as described. Matt got involved and together we learnt and mastered every aspect of eBay and how to grow a successful business.

Back then; running auctions on eBay was the most popular way to market your new or used products. During the first six weeks of our business, while studying and learning the ropes just from selling items from around the home such as clothing, shoes, purses, books, DVDs and even VHS video cassettes, we were making a net profit of between $600-$800 every week! Now, you may or may not think this is a lot of money by today's standards, however can you imagine our excitement especially after all we'd been through? To taste some level of success *finally* was thrilling to us. It restored the confidence I'd lost, as it was proof that anyone with the right knowledge and action could create an income on the eBay platform. We both knew without a doubt we'd find success this time.

Thanks to the credit we got from the bank, we invested another US$10,000 into one-on-one personal mentoring through a company in America to fast track our results and scale to another level. We were serious and wanted to make up for lost time. As always, we backed ourselves, and so did our mentor. Each week we'd have an hour with our mentor via telephone and he'd give us plenty of homework to keep us moving up the ladder towards success. Matt's dream of making $2,000 a week from the Internet was in our sights and for once I felt the same enthusiasm about the Internet as he did. At this stage we were still selling pre-loved items, however it was time to decide on our niche market and offer brand-new products to customers all over Australia. The best part was, if we sold a range of products over and over again, we could then automate some of the processes, which would free us to focus on scaling.

There were a number of ways to find products to sell online and one of them was to manufacture and import stock as it was easier to automate, and the margins were fantastic. Naturally, we had *zero* idea of how the manufacturing or importing process worked but we were willing to learn. Our eBay mentor suggested we hold back on the idea and try to find products within Australia, but *oh no*, I wasn't interested and wanted to go ahead with importing our own product lines. After six weeks of in-depth market research on eBay, we'd made our decision to go into the health and fitness category based on the numbers, which was perfect for me, as I understood it well and it was my true passion to help people. A month was spent reaching out via email to hundreds of suppliers in China, talking back and forth via Skype or phone, until I found the right one. It was so new to me, and without a mentor in this space I had to learn on the go and hope for the best. I was relying completely on my gut instinct. A silly and dangerous strategy, but that's what we did.

We could only afford two different items because we were using the credit card, so we decided on a spin bike and an elliptical bike for our first order. There were no documents or agreements in place and all I had to go on were dozens of emails, their website, and what the sales guy in China had told me over the phone. Matt decided we'd better fly to China to make sure things were in order before we went ahead with the order. We were on borrowed money and although we were careful, it wouldn't last long at the rate we were spending it. We booked our flights around the time the Chinese Canton Fair was on, so we could make the most of the trip. The suppliers name was Jerry and he'd arranged for us to be picked up from the airport upon arrival and driven to the factory to meet the staff and to view their products. The idea was to cement our relationship with Jerry and show we were professional and very serious about growing our manufacturing and importing business with his support.

We arrived in China and as promised a car was there to take us to our hotel and onto the factory. I don't know what I was thinking at the time, but I had on long business pants, a sweater and *high heel shoes!* Nothing wrong with the pants and sweater, but the *high heel shoes in regional China? WTF?* I hadn't counted on a three-hour drive inland where the roads were dirt, and it resembled nothing like I had imagined. We were deep in the heart of a province where high heels had no place! Matt and I were sneaking glances at each other in the back seat as the driver sped down the winding road to *God knows where.* He looked at me and I could tell he was wondering if we'd made a mistake. All of a sudden it started raining and before long, a thunderous sky opened up to torrential rain. The driver made no attempt to slow down, which made me grip Matt's hand in fear. *What was he thinking?*

The dirt roads quickly turned to slushy mud and still the driver didn't ease off the accelerator. Seriously,

FRUSTRATED TO FABULOUS

I was scared! Matt ended up telling him to slow down and he looked at us in the rear-view mirror as if to say, *What's your problem, we've got a meeting to get to?* I was beginning to wonder if this was such a smart idea, after all. I was busting to go to the toilet, we'd been driving for almost three hours by then, and I was over it! Finally the car slowed and pulled up out front of a massive building almost hidden behind an equally massive concrete wall. There was a small doorway, which indicated the entrance. It was still pouring rain and without an umbrella we stepped out of the car into inch deep mud (in my heels of course). We were hurried through the doorway and the moment we were on the other side, I could feel dozens and dozens of eyes upon us. They were the eyes of the workers in the factory who'd snuck over to see who the visitors were. It was as if they'd never seen a foreigner with blonde hair before. From what I could see through the rain, they were smiling curiously, which put me at ease.

In front of us was a set of stairs leading to the offices where Jerry our supplier and two ladies were waiting to greet us. He had the widest grin I'd seen for a long time. It was a big deal for factories to have visitors and they couldn't have been friendlier. The main office area was simple and clean and to the left of it was a big glassed-in room displaying about thirty pieces of different fitness equipment. Jerry couldn't wait to walk us around the showroom. He was beaming with importance. By now I was really busting to go to the toilet but glancing around the office I noticed there wasn't one. I signalled to Jerry I had to go and with a big toothy smile he nodded and directed the two ladies to accompany me. They both locked arms with me and walked me towards the door that lead back outside. For a moment I thought to myself, *Bloody hell, where are they taking me?* It was still pouring rain and one of the ladies held a flimsy umbrella above us while the other continued to nod her head leading me back down the stairs towards the entrance of the building.

As we got to the bottom of the stairs, to my right I noticed three outside latrines with no doors and a hole in the ground. They were leading me to the *toilet! Holy shit!* To my left were the workers who'd come forward again to stare at us. It was clear they didn't get many visitors. There were *no doors* on the toilets! By now the rain had caused mud gullies and potholes with water gushing everywhere. The ladies were trying to lead me towards the latrines with no doors. *Can you imagine it?* It's pouring rain, I'm in my long pants and high-heel shoes standing in inch-deep mud, and they want me to relieve my bladder in front of them and the factory workers, who seemed mesmerized with the whole scene! I practically froze in terror and crossed my legs, so I wouldn't wet myself. I turned to the ladies who didn't speak English but were trying to understand what my problem was. I was trying to tell them I had stage fright and I couldn't go in front of them and their workers! They didn't understand so all I could do was signal it was okay and I'd changed my mind.

Freaked out, the urge to go went away momentarily and with that I headed back to the office. The ladies looked at each other with surprise and I can only imagine what they were thinking. Upstairs, Jerry and Matt were discussing our first shipment after viewing the products, which we agreed were higher quality than we'd hoped. The hardest part was choosing only two items because of our budget, but we could see plenty of blue-sky opportunity, which made us excited. Most importantly, the boys seemed to have hit it off, as Jerry was still beaming and Matt was relaxed. Good sign. We were interested in a long-term business relationship, not a fly-by-night situation.

An hour later we headed out to lunch with Jerry who couldn't wait to show us around. I couldn't wait to get to the nearest toilet. Thankfully, the restaurant was just ten minutes from the factory and while the toilets were still holes in the ground, at least they were clean and had doors! We spent the whole day being chauffeured around enjoying every minute of it. We visited a piano museum, drank copious amounts of royal green tea, and learnt a lot about Jerry's home province and their culture. At the end of the day Jerry dropped us back to our hotel and while we didn't put an order in that day, we were certain he was the right supplier for us. The next day we headed to the Canton Fair to visit other suppliers and make our final decision.

Travelling to China to meet Jerry and visit the Canton Fair was one of the best decisions we made. We flew home a couple of days later and put our first order in with Jerry which was a 20-foot container, half being spin bikes and half electrical elliptical bikes. The total cost was US$9,000 and everything was arranged via email. We wired the initial 30 percent deposit to his company bank account and agreed the final 70 percent would be paid upon completion of the order. Thankfully he was extremely honest and respected us as clients because I had no idea what we were doing and without those documents and agreements, *anything and everything* could have gone wrong. Three months after we'd begun this journey, the first container arrived from China. We'd backed ourselves 100 percent and *nothing* could put a damper on our newfound excitement after what we'd gone through. We listed the two bikes on eBay and within weeks we'd completely sold out with a tidy profit margin of 35 percent. We celebrated like rock stars dancing around the apartment feeling like we'd won the lottery!

Up till this point we'd only shared with a few of our good friends what we were up to, after making a conscious decision to surround ourselves with people who would *not* pull us down or try to crush our dreams. As you can imagine, we had plenty of sets of eyes on us waiting in the background to see what we were going to do after they'd heard about our time in L.A. This time we were keeping things low-key, we'd learnt our lessons. We ordered our second, third, and fourth containers of fitness equipment, which had grown by a few different products within months and could barely keep up with demand. It was exhilarating! In fact, we grew the business so quickly we had to move storage warehouses *five times* over the course of the business. We were making more money than we ever thought possible within our first six months and Matt's dream of making $2,000 a week part-time was wasn't a dream anymore, it was our reality.

Eight months in, feeling over-confident, I ordered a full 20-foot container of electrical elliptical bikes, as they were our most popular item. Being naïve and not thinking professionally enough, I was still sending my orders to Jerry via email without the critical documents and agreements that would protect against disaster. The order was for almost US$30,000, a lot of money

FRUSTRATED TO FABULOUS

invested without proper agreements in place, right? The container arrived at the huge warehouse we were renting and all one hundred and seventy boxes were unloaded and stacked ready for sale. As expected, they continued to sell almost faster than we could keep up with demand.

It was heading into Christmas (and summer time in Australia), so as you'll guess, everyone wanted to look and feel their best. A few days later however, we started to get negative feedback in our eBay store and the phones started to ring with irate customers on the other end. It was the worst possible news and in a million years I'd have never expected it. Jerry had manufactured the whole container of electric elliptical bikes with European plugs attached instead of Australian plugs, which are totally different. *All one hundred and seventy bikes!* I nearly threw up as you might imagine. I went into a panic and nearly had a meltdown on the spot. I couldn't freaking believe it! My head was pounding from stress and we'd already sent out more than fifty of them to customers! This was very bad news for us and our valued customers who would be totally pissed off when they opened the box and saw the plugs were for European sockets. I got on the phone to Jerry and—trying to keep myself calm and professional—I told him what had happened. Naturally he was mortified and shocked that this had been "missed during production."

Missed during production?

Was he bloody serious? I could feel my heart rate increasing, for all the wrong reasons. Clearly, I was beginning to lose it and had to take a deep breath so I didn't yell at poor Jerry who I could feel was also stressed. *What the heck* was I to do? Jerry came up with the solution. He'd FedEx one hundred and seventy electrical adapters that would slot onto the European plug and fit into an Australian socket. I felt sick. My only other option was to send the whole container back to China, which would take more than a month and cost thousands of dollars. *That* wasn't about to happen. What a mess. I couldn't believe it was happening and I needed to make some fast decisions. We'd already sent more than fifty to customers and clearly some hadn't opened or received them yet because the phone calls from irate customers had just started that morning.

It dawned on me right then and there that it was my entire fault, because never once had I stepped up and asked smarter questions about the way I was conducting my manufacturing or importing business. I knew there was more to this process than back and forth emails and a whole lot of trust. How foolish I'd been. I was angry with myself more than I was with Jerry. He was silent on the end of the phone waiting with bated breath for what I'd say next. With a heavy sigh of surrender I told him to send the adapters at no cost *immediately*, which he agreed to.

Somehow, we managed to appease most of our customers after explaining our unfortunate situation and promising them a free, thirty-minute personal training consultation over the phone with me. Our income suffered as a result, but once we received the adapters from Jerry, we picked ourselves up once again, and kept growing the business, only this time, we'd pay the price to get our agreements, documents, and processes in order. Before long, we outgrew that massive warehouse and ended up buying our own as a business investment. There was so much stock, we needed a forklift to stack the pallets high against the walls and the shelves we had installed. Burnsy the cat would come to the warehouse everyday with Matt and me to get the sold items ready for shipping which sometimes took a few hours. It was the highlight of his day. Burnsy hated being stuck in the apartment because he couldn't get outside to do his wandering, so the warehouse was like his own playground. He was very popular with the neighbours and if he ever went missing we'd usually find him curled up in whichever warehouse had the most sunshine during the day.

One of the retail warehouses beside us sold Balinese furniture. There were two massive levels with all the beautiful furniture on display and arranged in detail so that if anyone came in to shop, they could see what it could look like in their home. The beds were made up beautifully, the cupboards and wardrobes displayed in an inviting way and stunning rugs had been placed all over the floors. Compared to our warehouse, which was full of boxes containing fitness equipment, theirs was spectacular. Burnsy thought so, too. He'd always wander into their warehouse, saunter around with a swagger as if he owned the joint, stopping for pats anywhere he could get them. Thankfully the owners were a lovely South African couple, who had moved to Australia and didn't mind him coming in almost daily—*not* that they had much choice. Burnsy was his own man and he went wherever he wanted, making friends everywhere with his loving energy and cutesy rolls. (I could write a book just on Burnsy and his crazy, unbelievable adventures, but perhaps another time.) Burnsy had to go to the vet for a deep scratch he had gotten on the side of his body after falling off some boxes in our warehouse. As cats do, he wouldn't stop licking and grooming himself, so he had to wear a plastic cone around his neck to break the habit.

The next day while Matt was preparing the sold eBay stock for shipment, the man from the Balinese furniture shop poked his head in the door and waved me over. He had a customer in his warehouse who wanted to purchase one of their display king-size beds upstairs but the problem was, Burnsy had put himself to bed and was snuggled up amongst the huge pillows, sound asleep with his cone on! Embarrassed but laughing, I had to go get him, which Burnsy wasn't too pleased about. The customer was amused with the whole scene and later the owner of the warehouse told me that Burnsy was his lucky charm and could come back anytime he wanted. Which he did.

The days, weeks and months passed quickly and by now we had our business down to a fine art. We hired a part-time assistant who took care of customers and administration and because so many of the daily eBay processes could be automated through the eBay platform, we were working two hours a day. Matt took care of the marketing and shipping processes and my role was to order stock and build out the product line. We had our systems down to a fine art, which were color-coded pink, blue, and purple jobs. We'd read so many business books and gone to so many seminars, and at last we could see the payoff that came with the sacrifices. We loved what we were doing, and it dawned on us that everything we'd written down on our dream list was now our reality. It also dawned on us that perhaps we hadn't allowed ourselves to dream big enough. We'd see.

We kept to ourselves as much as we could while building our business, but as you can imagine, friends and family began to notice changes within us. They could clearly see we weren't as broke *or broken* as we were after the L.A. trip. Some of them were genuinely wrapped seeing us finally get back on track, yet others laughed at the idea that we had an eBay business. We got comments such as:

"How's your little eBay business coming along Amanda?"

"Can you really make money with a hobby business?"

"Don't worry Matt, if this one fails you can always get back on the tools as a carpenter."

"Up yours!" Is what I *wanted* to say but of course didn't. We were so used to hearing other's opinions even though they had no clue about what we were doing, that in the end, we had to pull away from the negativity or ignore it. We began to notice that as it became obvious we'd found a way to start living our dreams, other people would compare their lives to ours and in an unconscious way try to pull us back to the level they were at. We never thought for a moment we were better than anyone else, but whom we were becoming as people from being mentally stretched, mentored, and educated outside of school was becoming apparent. We'd seen, experienced, and grown so much it was evident we had begun a true transformation. We needed to shed our old identities and catch up with who we wanted to be. For us, we wanted to continue our growth and see how far we could stretch.

Like you and everyone else, we had big, lofty dreams and if those dreams were to become our reality, we couldn't afford to let our thinking shrink to those around us who accepted an average life with no excitement, growth, or freedom. As old friends drifted away, new ones drifted in. Nothing was missing, we were just changing as people and it was *okay* by us. Some of our friends who genuinely wanted to know how they could change their lives and dare to write out and believe in their own dreams would come to our apartment to learn what we were doing. At first I was surprised in their interest, but thinking back, like most people they had a desire to live their dream life and have more control over things that mattered most. Matt and I happily talked about our plans for the future, always excited and eager for a grander adventure. I could see we were inspiring our true friends who made us feel good inside and if they wanted to follow us, they were welcome.

Almost a year later, our "little eBay business" was growing steadily, we were working on it around two hours a day, we had money in the bank, and life was good. Matt was surfing every day, I was running on the beach every day, we had great friends in our life and we had more free time than ever. There were so many things to be grateful for, you'd think we had it all. Problem was that while I was happy on the surface, underneath my gut was telling me something I didn't want to acknowledge, and the niggling wouldn't let up. I didn't know what it was yet, but something was missing, and I couldn't put my finger on it.

What was wrong with me? Why couldn't I just be content?

FRUSTRATED TO FABULOUS LIFE LESSONS

Okay Gorgeous, it's time to make a nice cuppa, take yourself and your journal to a quiet area for 15 minutes and write in *detail* your top three-to-five take-away *a-has* from my story so far and from the lessons that follow below.

Be Bold.
Be Courageous.
Be Fabulous!

This chapter holds plenty of tremendous life lessons which I know you'll relate to in so many ways, because it truly shows the power of what can happen when you write down your goals and dreams and take conscious and deliberate steps every day towards them. A valuable lesson here is the power in letting go of the past by learning to love *yourself more* and find ways to forgive and move on. I learnt a long time ago girlfriend, the past is history and it has absolutely nothing to do with the present or the future. At least twice a day write down things you are grateful for. It trains your mind to focus on positive aspects of your life instead of focusing on the past or things you do not want. The mindset mentoring we plugged into daily taught us that what we focus on, we bring on. This is important information for you to absorb and live by. This one golden piece of advice will change the course of your life if you follow it.

How often do you stop throughout your day and actually say out loud or write down, what you are grateful or thankful for in your life? Whether you are grateful for what you currently have or what you want, it doesn't matter, because your subconscious mind cannot determine the difference. It doesn't matter right this moment whether you believe me or not, just know that what I am sharing with you in every one of these chapters and life lessons is based on my own true experiences. Not one word of what I'm sharing with you is fiction and my hope for you is that you suspend any *disbelief* and see that for things to change, first you must change.

The reason I called this chapter "Careful What You Wish For" is because your thoughts, feelings, words, and actions become *things*. What you focus on, you bring on, in other words. As you see from this story, Matt got exactly what he wanted and a whole lot more. He got the income and the life to match and at the time he first said he wanted it, we had absolutely no idea of how we could make it possible. If your WHY is big enough, the HOW will come to you when you are ready. For us it came in the form of being able to tap into the power of the eBay platform. Yet in a million years if you'd have told us that we would have an eBay business, we would probably have laughed aloud.

Another incredibly important factor for you to consider today is, *Who are the people you surrounding yourself with right now?* Are they uplifting, and do they believe in your dreams as you do? Do they cheer you on or jeer at your daydreams? Be careful who you let in. Moving away from old friends, acquaintances, and even family members who pull you down can be difficult and in some ways painful, however you must ask yourself if the price you are paying is worth it. Don't worry, *I get it!* Over the course of our life together, Matt and I have had to detonate plenty of pullers out of our lives, but jeez it's been so worth it. And naturally there'll be family members you can't avoid, but our rule is that we see them less and *never, ever* share our dreams with them. If you must share your plans and dreams with others, make sure they have your best interests at heart. If you *don't* follow this advice, chances are your dreams will be shot down in flames!

Another tough lesson we learnt is that sometimes the people you think will be your biggest supporters will end up being the biggest pullers. This comes from greed, jealousy, fear, anger, and even hatred towards you. It's normal. I know, because I've lived it. But here's the thing. If your dreams are worth living, under *no* circumstances *and I mean none*, let their words of discouragement or resentment stop you. Think of all your heroes and imagine what they've had to go through to succeed in their lives. Are you willing to put yourself on the line and commit to your dreams? Do you know what you want out of this life? Do you have a nice, crystal-clear vision of where you're going? Have you written out in detail all your hopes and dreams with all the reasons why you must make them come true? *I hope so.*

Can you see from what I've been through that *anything* is possible if you have a dream and you believe in yourself? If you don't have goals and dreams and you lack confidence or belief in yourself, don't worry. I was once in your shoes but through the guidance and wisdom of mentors, I developed courage and learnt to be kinder to myself, and so can you.

Lean in on my strength and begin writing every dream you'd love to live, even if you can't see them becoming real just yet. In time, if you follow a formula I'll give you soon, you will see that you can make them *all* come true. Trust in the process and remember, you are worthy of a magical life, and I believe in you. ☺

FREE GIFT

www.gdaygorgeous.com/webclass

[8] THE BIG STAGE

"It is not selfish to love yourself, take care of yourself, empower yourself, and choose to live your life joyfully by design, not default, and never desperation."

—AMANDA JANE

THIRTEEN MONTHS INTO living our "internet" lifestyle that most people could only dream about, I couldn't shake off the restlessness I was feeling inside which made me feel guilty. *Something* was missing. Matt was happy as could be. He was surfing every day, had no money worries, and business was cruising along ninety percent on autopilot. We'd expanded our fitness equipment range and were one of the top three sellers in our category on eBay Australia. We were working around two hours a day. In fact, we were growing so fast we could barely keep up with sales and money was flowing in daily. A dream-come-true. You'd think that *surely* I couldn't hope for anything more, but oh no, it was never *that* simple. ☺

Out of the blue my mood changed, and I wasn't my usual up-beat self. Small, un-important things would bug me for no good reason and Matt seemed to be the one I'd lash out at when things didn't go my way. (Maybe *you* can relate to this?) As easy-going as he was, he wasn't into my mood swings and things needed to change. I explained how I missed being around people and the energy I felt when we had the personal training studio. As much as I loved being with him and Burnsy all day, it just wasn't enough for me. I wanted more from my life!

One of the many reasons I love Matt is because he never lashes back when I'm in one of my weirdo moods and always supports me in any way he can. A few days later over breakfast he said he had a solution for me, which was to create our own eBay home study course based on our personal story and importing products from China experience. This way I could get the connection with people I was craving and teach others how to use eBay as a vehicle to fulfil their own dreams and goals. My reaction was one of surprise and I told him I doubted anyone would be interested in his idea. But, I listened to him and by the next morning I bought into the idea because I saw it as a way to fulfil my dreams, which at a deep level was to connect with and help others.

FRUSTRATED TO FABULOUS

Still not 100 percent certain of Matt's idea or my ability, I decided to test the waters with a newspaper advertisement to see if there was in fact a market of people who wanted what we were offering. I'd learnt my lesson after the L.A. incident and never again would I take a product to market without testing its viability again. We ran a small advertisement in the *Sydney Morning Herald* newspaper, offering our whole proven eBay system, with personalized one-on-one mentoring for twelve months at an investment of $9,900. The reason I put a value of $9,900 on the program was because our eBay business was very successful. We had credibility, knowledge, and systems to support others in achieving their own goals and it was well worth the investment for anyone who wanted to shave years off their learning curve.

Not knowing what to expect from the advertisement I was shocked when the phone started ringing the same day the ad ran. We had at least a dozen calls from everyday people wanting to know what we did and how we did it. Surprised at the interest, I knew immediately Matt's idea was a winner. In fact, the very first gentleman I spoke with told me he wanted me to mentor him and he was ready to invest his $9,900 and begin as soon as possible. Problem was, we hadn't written the course structure and to tell you the truth I was shit scared at the thought! Mustering as much confidence as I could, I told him we'd need ten months to write the course and if he wanted to commit financially with a deposit, I'd be his personal mentor as soon as it was ready. He agreed to the terms, paid a deposit into our bank account, and waited for us to create the course. I have to say, his belief in our ability

119

to mentor him to success spurred us both into massive action!

As luck would have it (or is there really such a thing as luck?) in a previous job, Matt had put lesson plans and a training course together for a construction training company and felt confident we could create our own for eBay. Over the next ten months, we created a course that would deliver the structure, video, and audio lessons and information anyone could implement to create a successful eBay business. As soon as it was completed, I called the man who had responded to our ad in the newspaper and let him know we were ready. It was July 2006. He hadn't forgotten and was ready to begin. Through the home study course and our personal mentoring, he too found success, using eBay as his freedom vehicle. But the most exciting part was how much we loved the personal mentoring and seeing others reach their dreams like we were, following our systems and strategies.

In February 2007 I was given a golden opportunity to speak at a seminar and offer our eBay home study course to the audience. Even with my outgoing personality the very thought of being on stage in front of nearly four-hundred people staring at me freaked the crap out of me! The promoter of the event was the same company that had put the Internet seminar on in Nashville Tennessee all those years before where Matt had been rudely told he probably wouldn't make it onto their stage! *OMG!* The last thing I wanted was to be laughed at and judged if I stuffed up or forgot my words! Letting fear of rejection or failure get the better of me, I politely declined the offer even though it was

FRUSTRATED TO FABULOUS

my dream to mentor as many people as possible. Deep down I was disappointed with myself because I knew our home study course could really change people's lives.

The next morning the promoter rang me to say that if I didn't accept the opportunity to speak on their stage that day, he was going to bring a lady in from the USA to teach a different eBay course instead. Well! *That* comment certainly pushed my buttons. I couldn't believe the cheeky bugger, and what he shared with me next completely changed my life forever. He explained the audience was not there for *me*, they were there for *themselves* looking to find solutions to their problems, so if I could just *get over myself,* it would change my life and theirs. What could I say? God knows I was *so* scared, but I couldn't stand the thought of him bringing any other eBay speaker to his stage. I accepted his offer and had exactly four weeks to prepare a ninety-minute power point presentation that included an offer for our home study course. Diligently I worked on the presentation for hours every day in the lead up to the seminar, which was being held in Melbourne, Australia. *Talk about freaking out!* I was a mess during the final week leading up to it and how Matt put up with me, I have no idea! As always, Matt was 100 percent behind me. He believed in me more than I did myself, which was something I needed to work on. Actually, there were *a lot* of things I needed to work on, but one thing at a time!

Finally, the Saturday I was to present on stage rolled around and there were just fewer than four hundred excited attendees in the room, all looking for answers and solutions to their problems. Holding on to that thought was the *only* reason I wanted to get over my terror for public presenting, that and the fact that I knew I had answers to their questions. I'd walked in their shoes more times than they might have imagined. Matt took his seat at the back of the room to watch me and said he'd send me his best vibes and love. *Shit...*I felt as though I needed a bloody *miracle!* At exactly 1:45 p.m. the M.C. took to the stage to introduce me as the next presenter. Honestly girlfriend, I almost wet my pants I was so nervous. I was shaking and sweating as though I'd just been for a long run! Desperately I wanted out, forgetting why I was even there. All of a sudden, the crowd stood up and clapping loudly, welcomed me to the stage. I had on a baby pink skirt, matching jacket, and high-heeled nude shoes. As I hurried to the stage my feet were sweating so bad, my shoes were slippery inside and I almost lost my footing. I managed to keep it together and as I made it to the stage the M.C. handed me the microphone and said, "Do you know what this is?"

"Well," I said, "it looks like a vibrator but it's not."—Did *that* just slip out of my mouth? *Yes, it did idiot!* I said to myself as I prayed for the floor to open up and swallow me right then and there! Can you *believe* it? The crowd was silent for a split second, absorbing what I'd just said and then erupted into laughter. They knew they were in for a good laugh no doubt. *At my expense.* The spot lights shining on me from the back of the room where the audio was set up were blinding, and although I knew there were almost four hundred people in the room, all I could see was a sea of black for the first moments till I got used to it. *Holy shit...what was I doing up there?* I wanted to bolt off and hide. Too late for *that.* As my eyes adjusted to the bright lights, I

FRUSTRATED TO FABULOUS

could finally see the faces of the people. As expected, all were staring at me waiting to see if I could help them solve their problems. I tried to see Matt down the back of the room where he'd taken a seat at the speakers special table. There he was, sitting with five other seasoned speakers, interested to see how my first presentation would go. The pressure was immense.

With no choice but to keep going I tried to share my personal story but forgot what I wanted to say. I stammered, stuttered and got confused with my message so I turned my back to the audience and read my presentation from the massive screen above me, word-for-word because my memory wasn't delivering. There were sixty-three slides to get through in just ninety-minutes. I remember the pain as though it were yesterday. I tried my best to get into a flow, but it didn't happen. I was so nervous, my breathing was laboured, which affected the way I was speaking. I must have sounded as though I'd just run a marathon. At one stage one of my heels got stuck between two floorboards, which made me trip and leave my shoe behind. How *embarrassing*. Worse than that, I didn't stick to the *etiquette* and said a few things that I shouldn't have, which pissed one of the promoters off but got the crowd laughing and nodding. I could see him down the back pacing back and forth signalling to his partner his disapproval.

Shit…*there I go again. Always in trouble!*

I had no choice but to keep going. I was a sweaty mess. I could feel it run down my spine underneath my suit jacket. *Christ!* Why had I worn baby pink? Could they see the sweat stains under my armpits? Matt was watching me and even though he was a long way away,

123

I could feel him silently coaxing me along. He would have known I was in a world of pain and feeling out of my league. I was the new kid on the block and the only female speaker at the event. I'm *certain* I could feel the crowd's sympathy as they watched on, smiling their encouragement my way. Those smiles were all I needed to keep me going. I wasn't going to let the fear rob me of my one big chance to prove I could break through and not only change my life but change other peoples too. The words of the promoter kept coming to me: "It's not about you, Amanda. Get over yourself and think about how you can help others."

Twenty minutes to go and I knew either out of sympathy or empathy, I had won the crowd's approval because the energy had lifted and they were fully engaged, which tamed my nerves. As their energy rose, so did mine and all of a sudden, I was actually enjoying myself. Everyone leaned in and listened intently to the solutions I offered them to make their own dreams come true. Their presence was enough to get me to the end of the longest ninety minutes of my life. As I thanked them for their time and kindness, they rose from their seats and gifted me with my first ever-standing ovation. In that moment, my life changed forever, because how I felt wasn't about *me* for a change, it *was about how I'd made the people feel.*

As shocking as my first presentation was, it was one of the most joyful moments of my life standing on that stage seeing the lights go on for so many *life weary* people. I could see the hope and excitement in their eyes as they watched how we'd grown and changed our lives and how they could too, following our steps. As I was escorted from the stage, dozens of people rushed to me to shake my hand and show their support. They were laughing, asking questions and telling me I was "real and down to earth," which made them feel certain that if I could make it in life, so could they! By the time I'd made my way to the back of the room where the promoters and the crowds were, something inside me had shifted. Helping people change and transform their lives was truly my life's mission and if I could get over my doubt and fear of public speaking by focusing on *other people* rather than myself, I'd find the true happiness and fulfillment I'd been searching for. Thankfully the course was a hit and the promoters were pleased, although I knew I'd crossed the line a couple of times.

I mingled with the crowd for the rest of the weekend, listening to their stories of struggle and hope. Shocked at how many everyday people felt lost and out of control, it made me realize how deep my desire was to show them that if they changed their thinking, they could change their lives. eBay was simply a financial freedom vehicle at the time, however the message I wanted to get across was that true freedom and power wasn't in the vehicle, *it was in the mind.*

After that seminar, I was invited to do another, and then go on a tour around Australia as part of a speaking circuit. Loving the idea, I eagerly accepted because the eBay business was being run by our staff member, so we had the time and energy needed. After the first three or four seminars, being on stage sharing my story without Matt wasn't feeling right because he was half of our business. He knew as much about having a successful business on eBay as I did, and to be honest it wasn't as much fun going it alone because of the travel involved. We approached the promoter and he agreed it'd be good to have us both on stage, as there were hundreds of couples that wanted to go into business together at every event we spoke at. After our first trial run, the promoter decided Matt wasn't such a great speaker and it'd be best if we went back to me presenting on my own. We were both surprised and I was disappointed, but Matt let it go because he didn't want me to lose the opportunity to do what I loved, so he travelled with me and watched from the crowd.

A couple of months later I was presenting at a seminar with other incredible speakers, one being Dr. John Demartini who is one of my most inspiring mentors. He talked for an hour about how to live an inspired life through finding and living your purpose and mission. As I watched and listened from the side of the stage, I caught Matt's eye as he nodded as if to say, *Did you hear that?* I did, and it was during Dr. Demartini's presentation that Matt made up his mind that no matter how bad a presenter anyone believed he was, he was going to join me on stage so we could work and be together. From that seminar forward Matt joined me on stage every time and it was perfect for us. Before long, there were offers to present our course from five other promoters. As time went on our presenting skills improved and we spoke almost every weekend throughout Australia while still running our eBay business. We ran workshops for hundreds of our students three times a year in between flying around speaking on different stages and I have to say, these were some of the happiest and most fulfilling times of my life. Seeing and experiencing people's lives change and transform on a mass scale is truly the most special gift we could hope for from all the energy and effort

FRUSTRATED TO FABULOUS

we invested. Hundreds and hundreds of our students witnessed their dreams come true, and to see that we had such an impact on their lives is something I'll never forget.

In 2008 we presented in front of more than five thousand people in London, which was the biggest crowd of people we'd ever been in front of. Then in 2011 we had the incredible experience of sharing the stage with Robert Kiyosaki, Tony Robbins, and Donald Trump for more than four thousand people in Melbourne Australia. Sharing the stage with our mentors was incredibly exciting and then meeting them in person was a real highlight for us. Matt shared with Robert Kiyosaki that his book *Rich Dad Poor Dad* was the catalyst for us wanting to change our lives. Robert was so chuffed he called his lovely wife Kim over to hear our story. Both Robert and Kim said to Matt that just hearing how the book had changed our lives was worth every moment they spent educating others, which we understood because it was how we felt about educating our students too.

While 2008 and 2011 were pinnacle years for our education and speaking business; both these years were also two of the most disastrous for our eBay business, *and* our retirement block of land in Northern Queensland—Nothing could have prepared us for the news that was about to come our way.

FRUSTRATED TO FABULOUS LIFE LESSONS

Okay Gorgeous, it's time to make a nice cuppa, take yourself and your journal to a quiet area for 15 minutes and write in *detail* your top three-to-five take-away *a-has* from my story so far and from the lessons that follow below.

Be Bold.
Be Courageous.
Be Fabulous!

Again, so many life lessons to come from this chapter of life that I'm certain you'll relate to, especially that to live the life you dream about and absolutely deserve, you need to step out of your comfort zone and step onto your stage whatever this means to you. How did you *feel* as you read the part where I walked on stage for the first time in front of all those people making a fool of myself? Did it make you cringe? Did you feel sorry and felt glad it wasn't *you* in the spotlight? Or did you feel disappointed that maybe you didn't step onto *your* stage when given an opportunity? Remember the word "stage" is simply an analogy for you in the context of this lesson but think back over your life or even now. Are you living your dreams today or are you hiding in the corner hoping, wishing, and praying for something better?

If you could step onto your dream "stage" of life what would it look like? What would it feel like and what would it sound like? This is a great lesson because it gets you to step away from your current way of thinking and self-talk and takes you to a place of what is possible. One of my favourite sayings is, "I'd rather die knowing than die wondering." This quote has gotten me through some of the toughest times of my life when making decisions about whether or not to push past my fear and doubt and go for gold!

Life is about growth. If you do not grow, how will your *experiences* in life grow? Remember, we are just like trees, If we're not growing, we're dying! Being the master of your own life and destiny is about being able to make decisions and committing to seeing them through no matter the hurdles that no doubt will come your way. Learn to push past the fear and all the reasons why you believe you can't step onto your own stage in life because if you're not there yet, your excuses are just stories or lies you keep telling yourself. Can you imagine the fear I've had to overcome to end up on stage with my own great mentors like Dr. John Demartini, Robert Kiyosaki, and Tony Robbins?! In my wildest dreams I'd never have imagined this could be possible, yet by conquering the self-doubt, getting away from the naysayers, and empowering myself through constant and never-ending self-education, *look* what happened!

Jim Rohn who is another mentor says, "Work harder on yourself than you do your job, your career, or anything else in life." He means get a mentor, whether it's a person or from books, courses, seminars or whatever. Another thing Jim Rohn says that I *absolutely* live by is, "Formal education will earn you a living while self-education can make you a fortune." This is so true! And by fortune he does not just mean money. Any area of your life can be "fortunate," instead of dismal. You just need to make a decision and start with a plan immediately, before it's too late! The message is to invest in yourself or why would anyone else?

Right now, I don't know what your dreams are girlfriend, but what I *do* know for certain is that you too have the ability to step up and be the woman you were born to be. It is your duty to be the best version of you and shine your light on others. You too can be a beacon and give others you love and care about hope when there is no hope. Wouldn't you *love* that? That's true empowerment right there!

A massive lesson here is that who you want to become and what you want to do will determine what education you need to invest in to help you get there as quickly and pain-free as possible. This might mean taking a night class, engaging a mentor, an online course or community, a seminar, a book, DVD, audio, podcast, or even a mastermind group. Determine how much time, energy, and effort you are willing to invest in yourself and into reaching your dreams. You have come to understand through reading my story so far how much energy, effort, and self-education I have put into getting and living my dreams and we're not through yet but know this—There is nothing more expensive than a missed opportunity and now is your time to shine.

Write down in your journal every single thing you know you're good at or talented at or have learnt that others might want to learn about. Even if you're not sure like I was at the beginning, just write them down and as you continue on this journey with me, your mind will open to new possibilities and ideas that may change the course of your life forever. Or even if you don't want to share your wealth of knowledge like I do, write down all the things you'd love to learn and become talented at and go seek the right mentor that can start you on your journey. Who knows what's around the corner, but life is short.

You still have time, but remember, time waits for no-one.

FREE GIFT

www.gdaygorgeous.com/webclass

[9] Cups of Concrete

"Cherish your vision and your dreams as they are the children of your soul: the blueprints of your ultimate achievements."

—Napoleon Hill

DO YOU REMEMBER the Global Financial Crisis of 2008? *I mean who doesn't right?* Our American friends call it the Great Recession. So much heartache, so many stories of loss. I can only try to imagine the full extent of how this period impacted the many thousands of lives that it did in such a detrimental way. Like so many others, we also got

FRUSTRATED TO FABULOUS

caught up in the financial turmoil and had to take stock of where we thought we were at financially and face our new reality. Matt and I had invested our total life savings into an investment on a block of land from a developer. At the time we believed it would be our retirement nest egg. By being early-stage investors, we received a block of ocean-front land in the tropical north Queensland town of Cairns. It had been conservatively valued at over $1,000,000, which at the time was definitely more than we ever dreamed we would be able to obtain in our lifetimes working. The developer had also taken on funding for the project from a U.S.-based financial lending firm that was a major player in the lending of funds to developers in Australia and globally. The Australian office received notice from the head office that they needed to liquidate some of the loans and had less than 30 days to do it. If the developer was unable to refinance out of the loan in that time, they were instructed to call in the loan and repossess the equity. Usually the asset was land or buildings, depending on the status of the various projects.

As it turned out the developer running the project we had invested into was one of the companies required to refinance. And as the financial meltdown had begun, he was unable to secure alternative funding. The lender took possession of the development and everyone involved lost their money. I can remember very clearly the morning we finally got the news we'd been dreading. We were driving to the airport on our way to present at a seminar when we got the call that the deal had fallen over and that we were essentially penniless. That was something we didn't expect to experience ever in our lifetime, but there we were, back

133

to the bottom of the board of snakes and ladders yet again. Five years of hard work, saving every penny we could to be able to make a smart investment gone into thin air. Just like that. There was nothing we could do about it. We have never spoken to or tried to contact the man in charge of the development since. There was no point. He was an older gentleman and he was frail and broken as a result of the experience. He too had lost everything. Even worse for him, he was in his late 60s and felt he didn't have the time to recover. There was absolutely no point in blaming anyone. We had gambled and taken a risk without being educated enough to understand the consequences. For a number of reasons, we threw the dice and unfortunately the numbers we were hoping for didn't come up. Big mistake and an even bigger lesson.

After the loss of the land, which we honestly hoped was going to be a massive boost to our retirement, we had to take a good hard look at ourselves and decide what we were going to do. I think we both went into a bit of a shock as many other people during this time did. It was hard to believe the financial and personal devastation this crisis was causing. Compared to others, our loss may seem small, but to us, it was our *everything* at the time. We went through many emotions and hundreds of conversations trying to make sense of it all. We blamed others, we blamed ourselves. But that didn't make a scrap of difference. The result was the result and we had to deal with it. After weeks of wishing and hoping our property developer would work something out so we'd recover at least our investment, it became evident we wouldn't receive anything. It was gone. At this point in our lives we had two choices. We could easily wallow in self-pity and send ourselves crazy or even sick with anger and frustration, or, as I like to say, "have a nice big cup of concrete and find a way to get on with life."

We chose the latter. And I'll admit, without the mindset work we'd invested into ourselves over the years and having mentors to support us, we wouldn't have been able to pick ourselves up as quickly as we did and keep going. It was a *massive* financial blow, not only to our future, but also to our egos. Another failed adventure. Again, we were humbled and reminded that there was risk involved when investing into ideas or businesses we knew nothing about, or worse still had no protection or control over. Like history repeating itself, we kept the unfortunate news to ourselves out of sheer embarrassment, although there were so many others in the same boat. We decided to stay low-key and push on with our daily lives as if nothing had happened. Naturally, deep down we were hurting like everyone else who'd lost out, but no doubt there were tens of thousands of people from all walks of life that had lost more than we had. The negative news on TV was relentless and too depressing to watch, so we made a point of not listening to it.

For the next two years we dove into our work and between speaking almost every weekend and running our eBay business during the week, so we didn't have time for much else. We worked seven days a week, saving as much money as we could to make up for the initial investment we'd made in the lost land deal. Our next major, driving goal was to eventually have enough for a deposit to build our home. Our speaking engagements had ramped up and we loved what we were doing. Thankfully our work was our saviour. We grew our team by a few more people and moved into an office, which I swore I'd never do! But it was worth it. We had a lot of fun and focused on our students, who were really kicking butt with their businesses, and more importantly living their dreams. The emotional payoff we received as a result was what kept us forging ahead and on purpose. There was always so much to do and although we were sacrificing time with friends and loved ones, we knew it was necessary to achieve the goals we'd set for ourselves. We had a lot of catching up to do! For the next three years we filled our days with seminars, travel, workshops, customer care, our own eBay business, charity events, staff events, business, and TV media events—you name it, we were part of it!

We were getting back on top of things and the effort put in was paying off. There was nothing much to complain about and as time went by, we pushed the lost block of land incident from our minds, focusing on the present, planning for an exciting future. We'd finally saved enough money to secure a block of land to build our dream home on. This had been a dream of mine for the past twenty years. I actually had a big scrapbook filled with pictures I'd cut out of magazines, never imagining that one day I'd be lucky enough to be able to afford anything like what those pictures looked like. Both Matt and I loved the American Hamptons style of home and for years I collected magazines from airports we passed through on our travels, ending up with dozens of ideas. Inspired by possibility, I'd pour over that scrapbook for hours at a time, visualizing how our home would look. It was my birthday in December of 2010 when we actually moved in and to this day I still pinch myself with gratitude. I remember

FRUSTRATED TO FABULOUS

the day our best friend who we'd moved to L.A. with back in 2004 came to visit us, just after we'd moved in. As he wandered around our blue and white American inspired dream home, a tear of happiness for us came to his eye. He turned to me and told me that it was as though he was seeing inside that scrapbook I'd carried around for all those years. Then he commented that it was like walking into a big baby blue dollhouse and we just burst out laughing because it's what Matt says! Just goes to show the power of holding onto a dream. I'd stared at those pictures for so many years going over every detail that was only a dream for twenty years before it came to fruition.

One of the most incredible things about this home however, is that when we moved back to Australia from L.A. in 2004, we lived almost ten kilometres (6.2 miles) away. Six days a week I'd run along the beach starting from where we lived and always turn around at the half way mark at the exact street we ended up building our dream home in. Right on the sand at the half way mark was another grey Hamptons-style beach house. I loved it so much I would stand there staring at it for minutes as I caught my breath. I'd imagine myself living in my own dream home, although back then we were broke and living off the credit card. Every day and every night before we went to bed, we would write down twenty things we were grateful for. Whether we had them in our lives or not it didn't matter. No matter how big or ridiculous the ideas were, we'd write them down. The power of the mind and the power of your word can change worlds, as they say. Diligently and without question we did as our mentors taught and as time slipped by, one-by-one those dreams were turning into our reality.

Then January 2011 rolled around. Our eBay fitness equipment business was still in full swing until one morning we awoke to the news that one of the worst storms in fifty years or more had caused deadly floods. They happened so fast they ended up devastating many parts of South East Queensland and the state capital city of Brisbane. We watched in horror as the news on TV showed the devastation and lives lost during this tragic event. It was the worst natural disaster we'd seen in our home state, ever. The Brisbane River broke its banks and thousands of people lost everything they owned and for some, there was no time to evacuate. As of the 14th of January 2011, the floods had led to 30 deaths with many more people missing. The scenes on TV were horrific and extremely stressful to see. Matt rang my Dad and arranged for them to go up and volunteer their time and services, as soon as the roads were open and safe to travel on. It was the least we could do and from what we were seeing on the TV these people were in dire need of all the help they could get.

As timing would have it, only weeks prior to the floods, a full container of our fitness equipment had been moved to one of the first fulfilment facilities in Brisbane. The facility serviced different businesses all over Australia. They took care of inbound stock, shipping requirements, and customer care services. Problem was, their warehouse happened to be smack in the middle of the flood zone. We had only seen it once briefly and had *no* idea it was in the flood zone. Neither did they, apparently. Not only that, we hadn't yet organized any insurance for our container of stock, as it was still being unpacked and loaded into the massive warehouse. We were going to take care of it

FRUSTRATED TO FABULOUS

the following week as we always had stock insurance just in case. In the midst of this chaotic time, our eBay business was practically running on autopilot, which meant we were selling dozens of items every day. As you can imagine, our attention was *not* on our business as much as it usually was, but on helping our Brisbane neighbours in any way we could. Matt and Dad drove to Brisbane every day, doing what they could to ease the pain for others while I stayed back to continue running the business.

One of Matt's friends had moved his family into their brand-new dream home just six weeks prior to the floods but had to evacuate as the water rose up high and flooded their new home. The damage was so extensive, Matt offered the family of four our brand-new caravan that we had imported in from America just two months before. They were so grateful, and it was the very least we could do. For weeks after, Matt and Dad stripped the damaged plaster from the walls and helped get his home ready for massive renovations. At night they'd come home and the look on their faces were enough to see how bad things were in the flood zones.

Then, a week or so later we began receiving negative feedback in our eBay business with nasty, accusing comments because no one was receiving the products they'd bought and paid for. We were shocked because we had no idea our products weren't being delivered and I could see from the feedback we were in trouble. eBay, like Amazon, have strict rules and policies around customer feedback and care, *understandably!* We immediately rang the fulfillment centre in Brisbane and when no-one answered for two

139

days running; after we'd called at least a dozen times each day, we knew something was terribly wrong. After countless calls, finally one of the ladies that worked there answered the phone crying. She told us they were in one of the worst areas hit by the floods and everything had been wiped out. Through her sobs she explained almost every piece of our fitness equipment had been destroyed and there was nothing she could save. She couldn't stop crying and told us she had been left to sort the mess out. She had to ring all of their clients, to tell them the bad news and from her energy coming through the phone I could clearly tell she was at breaking point. I felt her pain as well as my own.

Shocked and devastated to hear this news, we immediately contacted every customer to explain why they hadn't received their fitness equipment. While most understood, we could do nothing to remove the negative feedback on our eBay account. As you might imagine, this would have a huge effect on the overall business. Because of the closed roads leading into where the fulfillment facility was located we had to wait a very long, stress-filled five days before we could go see what the damage was to our business. Matt, a staff member, and I drove to the area and what we saw was shocking. Thousands of peoples' lives had been affected and changed forever. The loss and damage was far greater than most had expected or could fathom—it was tragic. We drove slowly into the fulfillment centre and as we walked inside the stench of sewage and waste almost chocked us. I looked around at the devastation hardly recognizing the place. Walls missing, stock strewn everywhere, mud and silt covering the ground. Piles and piles of ruined products from dozens of businesses lay all over the filthy, muddied floors. It looked like a tornado had come through!

Looking around for assistance I saw only three staff that had stayed on knowing business owners wanted to come and ascertain the damage to our businesses. The lady I spoke to on the phone earlier in the week was the manager and again all she could do was quietly cry. She had no idea what to do or where to turn. For whatever reason, the owner of the company had left for New Zealand, leaving his staff to handle his clients and the mess. I remember feeling an overwhelming sense of sadness for the young manager who shared with me that day she was almost at breaking point. She couldn't cope anymore. I could see why. *It was a bloody disaster.* The three of us stood in silence staring at the wreckage of our fitness equipment. It was laid out all over the floor in massive lines. Hundreds of pieces of equipment soaked and ruined by the floodwaters mixed with sewage—Five years of work on our beloved eBay business along with our first taste of real success, all wiped out overnight.

Not being one to cry very much, I tried to put on a brave face because others had lost so much more than we had. Lives, homes, businesses, livestock, let alone everything else the floods had destroyed. Inside though, I was absolutely gutted, as nothing could have prepared me for what we were seeing. With no insurance, and no products to continue to sell online we were well and truly stuffed this time. There was nothing left, everything was destroyed. There was so much mud and silt on everything we couldn't even open some of the boxes to have a look. Not that we'd even consider trying to salvage anything. The smell alone was enough to turn the strongest of stomachs. I tried my hardest to be strong, but I gotta tell you, I was pushed to my limits and as the tears finally came and I stood there grieving for what was, I knew it was the end of our fitness equipment business.

Overnight we had lost close to *one hundred thousand dollars* in stock retail value with no insurance.

As if losing all our savings in the block of land in Northern Queensland wasn't enough, now this! It all hit me at once as I stood there sobbing feeling sorry for myself and for everyone else who'd been affected by the floods. My staff member, Genta, who'd been with us from the beginning of 2007 and loved the business as much as we did, felt the pain too and quietly walked away to give me a moment. It was the first time she'd ever seen me this upset. Cuddling me, Matt asked what I wanted to do about the fitness equipment business, as it was my baby in a way. My answer was that no matter what the outcome, we'd find a way to get back on our feet. We couldn't and wouldn't let this beat us. Another life lesson we had to receive and deal with. Again, we had two choices: wallow in self-pity or fight back and turn adversity into opportunity.

We had hundreds of students watching us in our community and I knew that through their strength, love, and support, we would once again recover. I wanted to send a strong message that with the right mindset, knowledge, community, and action, anything is possible. Right then and there, I made a promise to myself and our students, via a video Matt recorded on his phone, that we'd rebuild and come back strong. My intention was to turn this into a lesson for our students and not into a story of loss or reason to quit, which

FRUSTRATED TO FABULOUS

could have easily been the case the way I felt at the time. Two hours later, we drove away from the devastated warehouse with heavy hearts but also with sheer determination. The domino-effect the floods had on our business was massive. Not only did we have to fold the fitness equipment business, it meant the end of our business partnership with Jerry our manufacturer in China.

He was sad about the news and kindly offered us credit if we wanted his help to rebuild. As appreciated as his offer was, we declined. With no insurance and such a huge loss in retail value, I didn't have the heart to go back into fitness equipment again. It was time for a change. We never went back to visit the warehouse in Brisbane, they were too busy cleaning up the mess and in fact, they also had to close their business as no one would be game enough to leave stock there again. We gave them instructions to dispose of our wrecked stock and walked away from that business partnership too. There was nothing more either party could do. Apart from the stock we lost, we also had to refund all the money we'd collected through our eBay sales during those first days we hadn't realized the floods had wiped us out. Thankfully most people in Australia had witnessed via the news and TV what had happened, and just about everyone was super kind and understanding. Quietly we went about finding a new manufacturer for a new product range that had a lower investment level. After all we'd gone through over the years, we weren't about to let the last setback beat us down.

We continued travelling and speaking around the country sharing our story of inspiration with crowds of people and even though what had seemed like another huge financial and emotional loss for us, in many ways it was a blessing in disguise. Hearing our story gave so many people hope and encouraged them to keep on with their journey of achieving their dreams, no matter what life threw at them. Some cried, others laughed at our stories, but most of all I could feel their empathy and their respect for how we always managed to look on the bright side of life and keep a positive attitude. Without the seminars the support of our students and promoters, I know the road back would have been much harder. Every time we stepped on stage to speak and empower others who were searching for answers to achieve their own dream life, truly, *I* was the one receiving gifts of courage from them to keep going. Looking into their hopeful eyes as they watched us present solutions to their problems, I could actually feel their desire for a better life, which always made me want to be a better mentor and speaker. The better I became, the more I could give. That was my philosophy, anyway.

Even though the vehicles for wealth creation we were teaching were wrapped around eBay, the Internet, and importing their own brands of products, the real message was about personal growth and *empowering people* to be the best they could be. The true gift was helping them believe in themselves and that anything was possible with the right attitude and freedom vehicle. All most people wanted was to live life with more choice and freedom. Within three months of losing everything in the floods we launched a new eBay business in a completely different market. This time we went into health and beauty products for women and grew it into another successful business within eight short months. We had made a promise to ourselves and our students that we'd rebuild, and it sent an important lesson about the power of having purpose, self-belief, empowering education, taking massive action, and most important of all, *never, ever quitting no matter what!* Many businesses in the flood-hit areas were gone forever, but thanks to the Internet and our honed skill, we were able to rebuild and get back on our feet. Financially we lost a *lot* of money, but mentally we were fit and as challenging as this experience was, quitting and longing for the past was *not* an option.

Sadly, in 2012 our adored Burmese cat, Burnsy passed away from liver problems, which marked an absolute low point in my life. He'd had such a full and exciting life and had lived in *twenty-two* different homes, (no, not a typo) which most cats never experience. He was such a character and like I said, I could write a small book on his antics over the fifteen years we'd been lucky enough to have him in our lives.

From 2012 to 2016 we continued on with our speaking engagements around Australia, which kept us on the go yet fulfilled. Between the travelling, mentoring, running weekend workshops for our students plus running our eBay business, there was little time left for much else. However, we always managed to have fun, take care of our health and enjoy life to the full. Within that time, we also added three new additions to our family unit, two Burmese cats— Teddy Bear and Humphrey Bear. A year later we got a toy poodle by the name of Yogi Bear. They all got along superbly until one day out of the blue, Teddy Bear decided to move next door and never return. Our neighbour fell in love with Teddy, so we unfortunately had to hand him over as he'd made up his mind he wasn't coming home. Well, as they say, the cat is the master and will do as he damn well pleases! We often see Teddy sitting on our fence, but no way will he come inside. Thankfully Humphrey Bear and Yogi Bear are best of mates. Humphrey is Matt's boy and Yogi is my little sooky la la who lets me pet him non-stop which I love to do! We don't have kids of our own, so we spoil these two endlessly and they make our family unit complete in so many ways.

Late 2016 also marked the time that Matt was feeling ready for a change. He really wanted to develop affordable homes for first-time homeowners and investors but had been putting that dream on the back burner for years. To be honest I knew he'd wanted to get into developing property for years, but kept up the speaking engagements, travelling, and our own three-day workshops because I was truly living my purpose. As much as Matt loved our work too, we both had to admit deep down we both knew it was time for a new chapter in our lives. With heavy hearts we also decided that the following May in 2017, we would deliver our final seminar for our students which for me was letting go a big part of who I was. Even though that would be eight months away, for me, the grieving seemed to begin right away as reality sunk in. Because of this decision, it made sense to change our business model, wind back, and cut huge running costs. At the time, we had twelve staff members, an office, and a warehouse to consider. Over the next few months we wound our business back to the point where we closed our office and emptied and rented our warehouse. We also wound our staffing needs down to two amazing ladies in Australia, and one in the Philippines. The three ladies that still work with us today are Genta, who has been loyal through thick and thin with us since 2007; Grace who's been our main tech support guru since 2013; and my service-driven sister Carmel who's been on our team since 2014. Carmel's life mission is to give outstanding customer care to each and every one of our students, and let me say, she's incredible to say the very least! I feel blessed to have all three ladies in my life.

After we closed our office in January 2017, we all decided to work from our own homes and it's been the best decision of our lives. It has given us all more freedom and I love working from home with my furry kids running amuck and making the day even brighter with their constant antics. February 2017 came around too fast for my liking. It was time to prepare for our final three-day workshop for our eBay and importing students being held in May. It would be our twenty-eighth, three-day event, which had all been held on the Gold Coast, just near our home. These weekends were my absolute favourites. Hundreds of our students would come together from all over Australia and even New Zealand, America, and the UK. For three full days Matt and I would take them on a transformational journey of possibility. Our outcome was to stretch their imaginations beyond what they believed could be possible for their own lives. It was vital for our students to be able to learn in an environment conducive to their success, so they could meet and mingle with hundreds of other students all wanting the same outcome, as well as get to know Matt and me on a personal level. These events took at least three months of energy and effort to prepare for, so all of us focused on making sure our students got what they came for—peace of mind, clarity, next level business and personal education, plus a whole lot of fun!

You'd probably think that I was looking forward to this being our last three-day workshop as we'd made the choice for a life and business change, however I was far from feeling *that*. Matt was one hundred percent on target to go live his dreams of property development later in the year, however I was feeling anxious and very uncertain about how I could possibly fill the gap of what I was leaving behind. There was no time for worry though. We had a three-day action-packed show to produce and I intended it to be one to remember!

FRUSTRATED TO FABULOUS LIFE LESSONS

Okay Gorgeous, it's time to make a nice cuppa, take yourself and your journal to a quiet area for 15 minutes and write in *detail* your top three-to-five take-away *a-has* from my story so far and from the lessons that follow below.

Be Bold,
Be Courageous,
Be Fabulous!

FRUSTRATED TO FABULOUS

As you can imagine, writing *this* chapter brought back many memories I'd rather have forgotten. The lessons were tough, but the rewards we received for not quitting were golden. A massive lesson for us was admitting that "indulgence" had gotten the better of us when we invested into the land in Northern Queensland without having any insurance in place. We had no idea what we were getting ourselves into and we paid a huge price for being ignorant. Another painful yet fabulous life lesson was making certain we didn't stay trapped in the past of *what was* and finding ways to let go.

During *your* quest for the life you want, the universe will throw you massive and sometimes destructive curve balls you just won't see coming! However, when you feel defeated, beaten down, financially broken, mentally broken, physically exhausted, and completely *pissed off* with the world as I've felt many times, you gotta dig deep, harness your inner power, get back up, and keep going no matter what. This is the very reason you must work harder on yourself than you do anything else. If you don't condition your mental state and your attitude towards life, you will likely get beaten down and someone else will have power over you in areas where you do not empower yourself. The mindset conditioning and nurturing we've been gifting ourselves (yes, I call it a gift) since 1997 got us through the toughest times in life. Do you see how easy to it could have been for us to quit during those many times of adversity?

How do you handle adversity and times of absolute pain? Is your mindset conditioned to be able to pull yourself through the tough lessons life has a way of bringing you? That's especially necessary if you want to break away from your current situation for a better life or outcome. What are the beliefs and habits you've formed around how to act when things get tough? Do these beliefs and habits serve you or like most people, keep you captive where you are? Without a burning desire and dreams strong enough for living life on our own terms, we probably would have easily caved in from all the lessons we had to learn. Every day without fail, Matt and I would read our goals and dreams aloud to remind ourselves of why we could never quit, not at *any* cost! The sacrifices we made and *still do* are pale in comparison to the rewards we receive ongoing. This lesson alone is worth noting if you're wondering if it's all worth it in the long run. Hold strong to your dreams gorgeous, you're probably closer than you realize to actualizing them!

Starting now, picture yourself in a better position and steps closer to the goals you want to achieve. Make sure you're actually feeling good about them by chunking them down into bite sizes you can believe in and manage. As soon as you begin to feel inspired step into massive action constantly remind yourself of how you're going to feel once these goals and dreams start to be your reality. Give yourself the gift of time to feel the benefits and rewards because these thoughts will keep you moving towards the light even during times of darkness, I promise you.

An amazing lesson I learnt from the great Tony Robbins is that the "Masters of success (10 percent of all people) believe in their results before they see the evidence." On the other hand, "the masses (90 percent of all people) must first see the evidence before they can believe what's possible."

Which side of the "success" fence do *you* sit on? Would you love to swap sides? If so, keep reading. You will soon see the formula I live my life by. Because success is a way of life, you can see the pattern here of no matter how many times we kept falling down, somehow, we'd find a way to get up and keep going. You'll also notice that we made a pact or a point of not holding onto or dwelling in the past. It serves no purpose and what's the point anyway? Each of us only has the "now" so find ways to cherish and live in the moment when you can. Be grateful for what you have and more of the same will come because what you focus on expands. It is a natural law of our incredible universe.

Each of these experiences has caused Matt and me to expand in ways we never knew possible. So as unfortunate as some of them were, they gave us the belief that we could conquer any challenge, no matter how big or small. Best of all, our courage and willingness to continue expanding our minds was the gateway to a life full of purpose, possibility, and prosperity, and it can be yours too if you have the desire.

FREE GIFT

www.gdaygorgeous.com/webclass

[10] The Curtain Comes Down but Dreams Never Die

"When the voice and the vision on the inside is more profound, and more clear and loud than all opinions on the outside, you've begun to master your life."

—Dr. John Demartini

MAY 2017 WAS suddenly upon us. It was time for our final three-day eBay and Importing Mastery Workshop for 350 excited students, who were flying in from all areas of Australia. We always held them from Friday morning to Sunday afternoon at our favourite hotel, situated just meters away from the powdery white beaches and deep blue Pacific Ocean of the stunning Gold Coast, Queensland. Because we always have so many students flying in and staying for the three or four days, we wanted to make sure they enjoyed the beach, the ocean, and the surroundings each morning and afternoon. This way they had an opportunity to feel a sense of freedom, get invigorated, and open to learning as much as possible.

I've never been one for long, drawn out seminars, which our students liked because after all, we were teaching them about getting the lifestyle of their dreams by having an internet-based business, so we made sure they felt like they had the best environment conducive to learning and planning for their future. More importantly than just learning about eBay, manufacturing, and importing, the *real* magic for our students was their discovery of how they could rewire their minds to think like the masters instead of the masses. They all came for the same thing: freedom and getting a life on their own terms. Witnessing them breakthrough and realize that *anything* they could imagine was possible by leaving their limiting beliefs behind was always the biggest and most joyful accolade Matt and I could hope for.

I remember waking around 4 a.m. on Friday morning, which was normal for me, but this time even though I felt excited and full of energy, at the same time I was feeling a deep sadness inside of me. I tried hard to ignore it and pretended it was first day nerves which was still the case, even though we were about to present our twenty-eighth, three-day workshop. Truth being, these three-day events were the highlight of my year and this was to be our last. These events got me so inspired and in tune with our students' needs that I could literally present for ten days straight if given the opportunity. However, Matt on the other hand, after presenting for three days on stage was absolutely stuffed and felt like he'd run a marathon. Don't get me wrong, Matt cares as deeply for our students as I do, but he's more an introvert, whereas these events brought me alive and where I felt most fulfilled because I was living my purpose.

We arrived at the hotel Friday morning ready and hoping to transform lives at 7:15 a.m. as the doors were to open at 8 a.m. *sharp*. We ran a tight ship and our students knew it. The large crowd of enthusiastic students filled the hallways and as we gently nudged our way through, I couldn't help but notice so many eyes filled with hopefulness and anticipation for what was to come. Seeing and feeling their trust in us made me want to hug each of them and let them know that they didn't need to only trust Matt or me, they simply needed to trust *more* in themselves and understand that they *were themselves* the lucky break they were searching for. I made a mental note to talk about this because even though they *believed* they only needed education about business, what they truly needed *and deserved* was enlightenment about what was possible, once they let go of old beliefs, habits, language, and actions that weren't serving them any longer. Easier said than done, but if we could help them discover the power they each had within, that would be all they needed to go from a frustrating life to a fabulous life!

FRUSTRATED TO FABULOUS

At 8 a.m. sharp the doors were pushed open and over three hundred eager students rushed to fill the seats as close to the front of the room as possible. It was always this way, as though being close and in the presence of their mentors would make all the difference. And it did. Matt and I loved the vibes oozing from the eager ones because it filled the room with great energy, which led others to open their hearts and their minds. *Exactly* what was necessary, if we were going to transform lives over just three days! At 8:30 a.m. the workshop commenced as we were welcomed to the stage and as happy as I was, I already felt the dread of knowing it was our last. We made our way to the stage from the back of the room and the love and energy we felt as we moved through the crowd was palpable. I could tell this weekend was going to be a bitter pill for me to swallow because I was truly living my dreams, yet this was the last of these events.

As always, most of Friday was filled with teachings about human potential and breaking down the barriers that kept most of us captive in a life of frustration or desperation. We shared how most of us stay trapped in lives we don't like because of old habits and beliefs we learnt as infants and carry through to our adult years. We spent hours explaining and showing how it *is* absolutely possible to change these old ways if you are open, willing, and have a massive desire to do so. The reason we spend valuable time talking about this is because it's of no use to our students to learn *anything* about making money or business, if their mindset is set for failure, fear, suspicion, disbelief, anger, unworthiness—*you know,* the whole parade of fear-based stories we tell ourselves that keep us mentally poor! Or even worse, fear-based stories that *others* tell us, that keep us mentally poor!

Argh! I get worked up talking about this, girlfriend, because until Matt and I made it our business to understand how we are wired, we too were living with the idea that we could never have a life we only dreamed about. It's just not true. From my experience, you can!

As we delved into the subject of personal empowerment more and more, I watched their faces, feeling their energy. The deeper we dived into giving the knowledge we knew they needed the most, the more surprised, saddened, angry, or inspired they became. What's incredibly interesting about all this, was watching peoples' faces as they listened and filtered what we were saying. Some loved it, others hated it, understandably. It's as though we're ripping off Band-Aids that had covered wounds for years and years. It's as though I could read their minds, watching their faces from the stage. What's most incredible is the fact that often the people who needed to know this life-changing information the most, were usually the ones that got pissed off with us and asked us to, "Get on with the business stuff." Interesting isn't it?

"This *is* the business stuff," I'd say. "The business of *you!*" And we pushed on anyway because I knew that we'd be doing them a disservice if we brushed over the most critical component of what it takes to become successful in all seven areas of life. And like Tony Robbins says, the masses (90 percent of people) must "see before they believe," whereas the top 10 percent (where all the success and wealth sits) "believe before they see." Knowing this makes it obvious to me that without this component of learning, how *could* it be possible for our students to even hope for success in any area of their lives, let alone make money and wealth through business? As mentors, standing in front of our students on that stage, we had a moral obligation to not only give knowledge of some of the whole picture, but to *give the whole picture,* so that our students have the best chance at fulfilling their dreams, *no matter how big or small they were.* By lunchtime, we were well into what I like to call the "transformation" process. It was our mission to give our students every piece of evidence and advice, based on our personal journey, which they could implement into their own lives to reach their outcomes faster. We had fun, tons of interaction, listened to dozens of interesting life stories and took time to personally meet and talk with as many of our students as possible.

Always without exception by the end of the first day of the event, we could see a shift-taking place from within so many people. Finally, the curtain of lies they'd been told or told themselves, and the idea of conformity had been pulled back to reveal a life that could be as magical as they could dream it to be. Standing there on stage at the end of the first day I knew deep inside that shining the light of truth on our community and seeing the "lights finally go on" for them could be enough to get me out of bed every day for the rest of my life. And before we knew it, the first day had come to a close. As our students filtered out of the seminar room and after receiving dozens of hugs and kisses, born from sheer relief at what they'd learnt that day, I was feeling fabulous but also a little heavy-hearted because it was the last day that I would get to teach my favourite subject in the world, *personal transformation. It's the elixir that could and would set someone free of frustration and entrapment if they had enough desire.*

All the rest of what was to come over the next two days would be mainly wrapped around wealth creation, eBay, manufacturing, and importing. And although these are the main subjects we knew our students had travelled to learn more about, I knew they'd already gotten what they *truly* needed that first day. By 8 p.m. as usual, I was in bed ready for sleep, yet my mind was racing a hundred miles an hour. Call it nerves, excitement, surplus energy, *whatever,* I knew it was something else. There were only two days left of the event and I *didn't* want it to end. There was so much left in me, and so many people that were hungry for the knowledge and wisdom we possessed because we'd walked in their shoes in some form or another. I didn't mention a word to Matt because I didn't want him to feel guilty or try to fix how I was feeling. There was nothing to fix, anyway. I just needed time to adjust. Well, *that's the lie* I told myself anyway, and as I turned off the light I prayed I'd get to sleep fast so I could shut the inner chatter down and be fresh for tomorrow.

Next morning, I was wide awake at 4 a.m. ready to begin the day. The inner chatter was in full force telling me I'd made a big mistake and was giving up my life purpose and mission I was meant for. But it was too late, Matt and I had agreed it was time for a new chapter on this grand adventure we call life. Quietly and quickly I got ready for day two. We opened the doors at 8:15 a.m. to a sea of people but this time, the energy was different than it had been this time yesterday. It was more uplifted and the chatter amongst our students was loud and filled with excitement in comparison. The day before had been a day of awakening and no doubt we'd opened their minds and hearts to possibility and ideas they'd never considered before. It seemed that some of our students were dancing on clouds as though they'd had a massive burden lifted from their shoulders. After settling in and answering dozens of questions related to the previous day's content, it was a time to learn new ideas and strategies that would set them on the road to fulfilling their dreams, if they chose to implement following our footprints.

The day unfolded exactly as planned. By lunchtime new lifelong friendships and alliances had been formed between our students, which boosted their confidence even higher. We too had made many new friends and although they were our students, our respect and admiration ran deep. We too are *always* students of life, no matter if we were on the stage or sitting in the crowd. Saturday night was a special night as it was tradition for two hours after wrap up at 5 p.m. that we'd mingle with our students over a casual drink or two, just so we could get to know them and also give them an opportunity to ask us as many questions as they'd like. Some of the stories of what our students had experienced on their life journey blew my mind and it made me respect them even more. Some of them had been to hell and back on their quest for a better life, yet still had hope and that's why they were there. Others told us that coming to our three-day event was their "last resort" and if they didn't find success after *this* weekend, then in their minds *nothing* seemed possible. When I heard these sorts of statements, I always reminded them that *they* were the answer. They just needed help seeing it.

Story after story was told and listened intently to. Some of them said that no one took the time to listen to them or believe in their dreams and that coming to this event gave them courage to keep going towards a brighter future. So many stories, so little time left before the event would wrap at 5 p.m. Sunday. At 7:30 p.m. we snuck away from the crowd who were still mingling. We drove home in silence, both of us deep in thought. Sunday would be the final day of our *final* three-day event. Some of our students had joked that night with us saying we'd be like the famous musician, John Farnham, who made a number of comebacks after his departure from stage, but that wasn't going to happen. *At least* for Matt anyway. Exhausted from another massive day we fell into bed and again I had a restless night tossing and turning. The stories I'd heard kept playing in my mind. The smiling, hopeful faces of our students clear in my mind's eye.

Sunday morning, we arrived at the event at 7 a.m. so we had extra time to mingle and prepare for the opening at 8:15 a.m. Crowds of people were already lined up, talking excitedly and waiting for our arrival. They sure were keen! As soon as the doors pushed open at 8:15 a.m. a bunch of students rushed to the stage to give their final hugs and well wishes before the day's end in case they didn't get the opportunity at the end of the day. Some even had tears in their eyes knowing it was the final time we'd all be together in one room where all the magic seemed to be. I certainly wasn't expecting *that!* The morning flew by and as day three began to fly by, you could feel the electric energy fill the room. Faces were beaming with emotions running high. This was not your *everyday* seminar and I believe it's why we were lucky enough to do 28 of

FRUSTRATED TO FABULOUS

them, over the twelve years we held them. One of the many highlights at each of these three-day events is that through the generosity of our students and us, we raised money for one of our favourite charities, The Starlight Children's Foundation, which is a non-profit organization for kids in hospital and their families. The programs offer entertainment, education, and technology to critically, chronically, and terminally ill children.

At 11 a.m. as always, a Starlight representative joined us on the stage to play a video and thank our students for their kind contribution and to show how their money is used to support the kids and families in need. One of the reasons we supported this wonderful charity is because quite a few of our students have needed the Starlight Foundation's support themselves. And when we talk about the importance of giving, it really resonates with so many. I'm extremely proud to say on behalf of our students and our business, that over the years the donations reached an incredible AU$210,000, which we know has supported so many families through very difficult times. And if you're reading this and you are one of those thousands of contributors, then *THANK YOU GORGEOUS!* I must say too, that every single time the Starlight representative plays the videos, showing the kids and the families and the challenges they're going through, there's never a dry eye in the room afterwards. It has such an impact on each of us and it certainly makes us all more appreciative for our general health. As the Starlight lady left the room at 11:30 a.m. holding her check for AU$6,000, it reminded me that this would be the last time our community of people collectively would make these contributions.

161

AMANDA JANE CLARKSON

Over the twelve years we always raised between $6,000-$10,000 at each event, which is massive when there's only a few hundred people in the room, which goes to show how big the hearts are, of our people and why we appreciate them so deeply.

The afternoon flew by and before we knew it, it was 4 p.m. Sadly, it was time to close the seminar out and say goodbye to an era that had transformed our lives forever, as well as the lives of thousands of people who'd been inspired by our trainings to transform their own lives. So many memories, so many stories. Dreams, goals, aspirations, reasons why, everyone attending for their own outcome, but *all* were there to learn how to live life on their own terms. Looking back, I would say this final day on our own stage was one of the low points of my professional life. Here I was wrapping up a part of my life that had not only given me more than I could have ever dreamed of and made me who I am today, in that moment I was wrapping up and saying goodbye to a part of me that was *truly still alive* with so much more to give. I was *already* living and giving my truth. *Now what? God, I felt like bursting into tears all of a sudden but kept smiling as though nothing was amiss even though my eyes would have spoken volumes.*

As we called to the stage our staff and volunteers who'd worked tirelessly for months to put each event on, it hit me that *this was it!* Tomorrow morning I'd wake up with no more seminars or workshops to look forward to. We thanked our students for taking the time from their busy lives to attend this final event for their own making. And without each of them, our work would not be possible and for this Matt and I are truly thankful. The crowd jumped to their feet clapping, cheering, and whistling loudly, giving us and our team

FRUSTRATED TO FABULOUS

the best farewell they could muster. Emotions were high for our students and us. Tears welled in my eyes and it was a struggle to contain them. In the end I didn't bother trying to hide my emotion, it was how I felt and by then everyone knew me pretty well. Our mission for this segment of time and space was almost over, but something was telling me I'd be back in some way. How could I possibly take a bow and walk away from people who clearly needed leadership, support, encouragement, a guide—*all the tools* required for living a life of success? Well, I didn't have the answers right then, but as the final curtain came down, and our students made a beeline for the stage, I prayed the answer would come soon.

For the next six months, we were busy taking care of our students who were continuing their mentoring and education journey with us. As part of their online private program created especially for them, included is a bi-weekly live one-hour video question and answer session with Matt and me. We call it the Hour of Power Mastermind Session and without exception, these calls are the most powerful form of mentoring as each individual feeds off the energy and brain power of the others. This means more potent solutions and faster results. We haven't always mentored our students this way, however over the past few years we've found that it's the smartest way for everyone to interact and be part of something bigger than themselves, *plus* it's the closest feeling to being in a room together, where we can mastermind each person's business and their personal growth as a collective. Each fortnight both Matt and I would look forward to seeing how they were progressing, but more importantly, what transformations in their personal lives were taking

163

place, and specifically which goals they were achieving. The bi-weekly live calls are definitely a highlight of my week and have been for years, however the final event was the last intake of students who would get this type of "closed door mastermind mentoring." It would appear we were mainly "eBay or Importing and Manufacturing" business mentors, but indeed, I'd say more like "Life Success Mentors." At the end of the day, the *ultimate lifestyle* our students wanted to create by becoming the person they wanted to be, was *ours and their* main focus.

By December 2017 which was just seven months after the final event, Matt was living his perfect day. He'd get up, have breakfast, go for a two or three-hour surf at the end of our street, come home and do four hours work on whatever property project he's into—*Finally,* he started doing what had been his dream for the past five years. On the other hand, I was feeling a bit empty, which is *so* unlike my usual self. Matt suggested countless ways I could fill my days, and even suggested I consider retiring and chill out for as long as I wanted. As sexy as this may sound for some, for me it held *zero* appeal. Don't get me wrong girlfriend, as much as I love to have fun and chill out, I'm not quite ready to hang up my high heels just yet, LOL! But seriously, the fulfillment I feel for presenting transformational education and mentoring our students on a larger scale was what was missing for me. As much as I tried to fill the gap with other business ideas, nothing seemed to suffice unless it had *anything* to do with helping others transform their lives as we had. There was only one answer that made sense with all the turmoil I felt at the time. We ended up taking the whole summer off, so I could sit, think, and just *be.*

I needed to decide what was right for me and not rush into something that wasn't going to match my highest values.

In March 2018 One of my mentors who knew me like the back of her hand as I'd been seeing her for five years, suggested countless times I should be writing a book about personal empowerment and to take my wisdom and knowledge to others who were seeking to reach their own dreams and a life by design but not knowing how or where to begin. Actually, she's a very wise, spiritual being, and had been on my case for three years about this very subject, yet I refused to take her advice. Too hard, and besides, I already *had* a business for God's sake. Of course, she already knew this, but every time we got together for a session she'd tell me I was meant to do transformational and personal empowerment work teaching others from my experience, *whether or not* I wanted to listen. As soon as she suggested it again in April 2018, my first thought was, *No way!* Not because I didn't what to inspire or impact others, but because the whole idea sounded too much. *Bloody hell, what was she thinking! Maybe Matt's idea about retiring was a good idea after all?*

Then, in May 2018 my best friend and mentor invited me to present at his Amazon summit teaching people how to manufacture and import private label products from Mainland China, which I've been doing successfully since 2005. I immediately jumped at the opportunity knowing it was a perfect fit for his people and my experience. There were more than 1,000 people attending the summit and I felt excited for the day to arrive and be around the familiar energy I loved so much. I remember walking into the massive ballroom that had been set for the 1,027 attendees the night before I was to present. I wanted to get a feel for the room and walk the stage while the room was empty. It was a little tradition of mine that helped prepare me mentally, so I could bring my best self on the day that mattered. There were people mingling outside the doors and even though it was the night before the event began, you could feel the positive vibes and electricity of their energy in the air. I loved it. I smiled their way, feeling their eagerness as a guard led me into the grandly set room. As I stepped inside and saw the massive screens, the tables set, everything in place a wave of belonging washed over me. The guard stood by the doors watching, as I wandered through the room and made my way to the stage. I wanted to imagine myself standing in front of the people, sharing my wisdom and giving the best of myself because they deserved nothing less.

I walked from side to side and back to the middle where I stood looking into the space that would be filled with knowledge hungry people the next morning. As my stomach did a little backflip from enthusiasm not fear, I realized in that moment my work here, was *far* from done. As I headed back to my room to prepare for my presentation, a few of my students who were attending the summit for the second or third time approached me, to see if they could ask questions and take photos with me. It was always a highlight for me to hear their stories, answer their questions and give them the encouragement they needed to keep going on their quest for success, as I knew intimately the exact road they were embarking on. I'd walked thousands of miles in their shoes since leaving home at sixteen on my own quest for freedom and success. There wasn't going to be much they would experience that I hadn't in some way. I was sure of it!

The next morning, I arrived early to see hundreds of eager attendees lined up waiting to enter the summit room. All buzzing and talking about their businesses, their dreams, their problems, their concerns, their wins and losses. The energy was electric to say the least and I felt even more charged as a result. At 11:15 a.m. I was introduced to the stage and I couldn't have felt more at home, relaxed, and ready to give my best. For the next ninety minutes I engaged the audience, educating and empowering them to believe in themselves and showing by example, that if I could find success in business and life, then so could they. At the end of the ninety-minute session I was swamped with people telling me that my story gave them even more courage to never quit on their dreams and just go for it. Hearing so many stories from people from varied backgrounds was reassurance that I wanted to continue on my mission to empower people, but not just in business, in all areas of life.

The weekend flew by and as the Amazon summit closed on the afternoon of the third day, I made a promise to myself that I would take some time to really think about how I could impact and empower more lives based on my own stories, experience and wisdom. I felt *alive* just thinking about it! Keeping my promise to myself, the next week I booked myself into a hotel for six days and five nights, so I could do some deep *soul searching*, you might call it. I wanted to have *zero* distractions and spend time alone to decide on how I wanted to live the rest of my life. Matt was all for it and took care of everything, so I could have the time I needed and as you can imagine, he wanted me to be happy! He has a funny saying you may have heard a version of:

A happy wife means a happy life.

Over the next six days I mapped out how I wanted every area of my life to be, in detail:

1. *My health,*
2. *relationships,*
3. *vocation,*
4. *money,*
5. *personal empowerment,*
6. *love,*
7. *and happiness.*

I thought about what I wanted my perfect day to look like and whom I wanted to spend my time with, because for me, time is the *most valuable* commodity, of which we cannot get more of, once spent. I wrote out the types of people I wanted to surround myself with, and what types of relationships I wanted to foster, now and into the future. I wrote about every area of my life, including if I did create a community for empowering women, what would it look like? So many ideas, so many breakthroughs occurred in my little hotel room and to be frank, I'd encourage you to take a day or so out for yourself and just *be* instead of *doing* for a change too. Anyway, on the fourth day I had another big breakthrough and decided to begin writing a self-empowerment book, a *guide* really, for women who dared to live their goals and dreams, based on my true-life story. A book which my mentor had been on my case about, for three years! It is the very book you're reading right now girlfriend and as I sit here typing this

FRUSTRATED TO FABULOUS

sentence, I am sitting next to Matt on a sunbed in Waikiki, Hawaii, overlooking the infinity pool that blends into the stunning Pacific Ocean. Life is good, and I'm feeling blessed right now. I appreciate you reading this story and hope you're *fired up and inspired* to go for your goals and dreams as a result. I wanted to turn our holiday into a sort of working holiday and finish the first draft of this book, because I must say for me, Hawaii has a sort of magical essence about it. So for the past seven days I've been enthusiastically writing for hours at a time. *I hope you're enjoying these lessons as much as I'm enjoying writing them for you!* And as I said, on the fourth day I began writing this book and by the end of the sixth day, I knew what I wanted and needed to do once it was complete.

Matt came to pick me up from the hotel and as soon as he saw me he knew I'd had the breakthrough I was searching for. My energy had shifted, and I explained to him what my intentions were moving forward, and how I wanted to empower and affect women globally, especially those who dared to live their dreams but wanted to be part of something bigger than themselves—A mastermind of like-minded others who understood them, and a mentor who'd walked a thousand miles in their shoes, and knew how to support them on their winding journey. For the first time in at least six months, I was finally feeling like I'd had a heavy weight lifted from my shoulders. I knew deep in my gut that I'd made the right and wise decision for myself, because the day I started the book was the day my inner chatter became quieter. It was as though my inner guidance had finally won out once and for all. Every morning since, I awake at 4:30 a.m. and begin writing by 5:30 a.m. as the sun comes up.

169

Although it's not my normal practice, I have devoted my mornings to writing until it is complete. I am committed and disciplined, for this work is *too important* to leave to chance. It's now the middle of June 2018 and as I finish this chapter about my life journey, here in breathtaking Hawaii, the sun is setting over the beautiful ocean. Tomorrow is a brand-new day and I'm eager to write the last chapter of *Frustrated to Fabulous* because it isn't only my story, *it's more about you.*

We're *finally* ready to delve into my LIVE NOW Freedom Formula, which is the acronym I live my life by and you can too if you choose to. Right now, moment-to-moment is all the time we *really* have and what counts. The past is forever gone and the future uncertain. The LIVE NOW acronym which I'll break down the meaning of letter by letter, reminds us all how precious time and life truly is. You will see that if you follow my guidance and let yourself believe that the impossible can be the possible, you will begin to transform your own life, and experience magical changes within yourself and the world you live in. In other words, you can set yourself free from a life of feeling frustrated and out of control in any of the seven areas. You can be, do, or have anything you choose. But if, and only if, you are willing to follow and implement LIVE NOW Freedom Formula success principles.

FRUSTRATED TO FABULOUS
LIFE LESSONS

Okay Gorgeous, it's time to make a nice cuppa, take yourself and your journal to a quiet area for 15 minutes and write in *detail* your top three-to-five take-away *a-has* from my story so far and from the lessons that follow below.

Be Bold.
Be Courageous.
Be Fabulous!

Writing this chapter was by far the most emotional for me, as it brought back so many memories that shaped my life into the woman I am today. The rollercoaster I felt as I relived the story had me in tears of sadness and tears of joy, which I know you'll understand in some way, when you compare the story to chapters of your own life. Especially if like me, you've ever sold yourself out and kidded yourself that your own dreams don't matter or that someone else's dreams are more important than your own. The six months I tried to fill the gap of how I felt after our last three-day workshop was probably the most frustrated I'd felt for years. I had an emptiness in the pit of my stomach that nothing seemed to fill, no matter how many lies I told myself.

Can you relate to what I'm saying in anyway? Have you tried to fill a gap within yourself, knowing deep-down you were born for so much more than you're doing with your life right now? Have you also been lying to yourself, showing up each day living your life around someone else's goals or dreams instead of your own? What are *your* life's goals and dreams? Are you living them or on the way to them right now? Can you still *see and feel* them clearly and read or look at them many times a day to keep you focused and disciplined to reach them? And if you're at a time in your life where you're wandering around worrying about the next phase of your life like I was, the lesson for you here is about finding the gratitude and peace in *what was* but shifting your focus to what will become. Always be focused on the present and planning for the future. The past is history and from my experience, there is zero point in looking back and wishing it were different. When things come to an end, whether it's in your personal life or professional life, it is up to you how you view the situation. We all have a choice.

We can learn to make peace with it and make a conscious effort to focus on new beginnings or we can dwell on and live in the past with regret, anger, frustration, hatred, jealousy, and all the feelings that can never help us move forward. Easier said than done, I know, but over time it can become easier, with practice and patience. This is what the next chapter of this book is dedicated to, giving you the tools that will take you away from feeling frustrated with your life, if you use them. You see, all the experiences we have in

FRUSTRATED TO FABULOUS

life add up to who we become as people. We all feel pain, loss, sorrow, anger, bitterness, jealousy, and all the other negative thoughts and emotions. However, staying with any of those feelings or thoughts for long will only bring other debilitating, matching thoughts and experiences of the same.

With all your strength and focused energies, you can write a new chapter in your life, if you're not being the woman you were born to be. *Yet.* Tell a new story using new words beginning today. It doesn't matter what area of your life you focus on—health, relationships, money, personal empowerment, vocation, love, happiness—whatever you're feeling is missing, begin there. No matter where you're at right now in this moment, you have the ability to move a step closer towards your goals and dreams no matter who you are or where you've been. I know this is a true statement because I have experienced immense pain, loss, unworthiness, confusion, disappointment, loss of identity, and all the other negative emotions we feel as humans. But I also know that each time I went into those darker areas of my mind, by consciously focusing on what I did want in my future, not what I didn't want, I have always pulled myself quickly to a brighter and more hopeful space.

How you let your mind wander or not, is up to you, but if you choose to you can focus and look forward to the bright, meaningful life you were born for, by taking time out as I did to *think* and *be* instead of just *doing* all day long. All you need is a few hours, or if you can take a day, take it! You deserve it. And you saw how powerful this exercise was for me. I found peace by writing in detail how I wanted every area of my life

173

to be, and now it's your turn. Remember girlfriend, you are never too old or too young or too *anything* to learn new things. Be open, be willing, and have the attitude of a *master* of life, one who has the ability to *believe in her results* before she *sees the evidence.* I promise you, that if you shift your thinking by taking new actions daily, you will transform into the woman you want to be, and your life will be even more fabulous with endless possibility.

Follow me into this next chapter of your grand new adventure, and you will see.

FREE GIFT

www.gdaygorgeous.com/webclass

PART TWO

YOUR LIVE NOW FREEDOM FORMULA

[11] Your LIVE NOW Freedom Formula

"The basis of life is freedom, the result of life is expansion, the purpose of life is joy."

—Abraham Hicks

BEFORE I GO ON, I must share something very personal and very emotional with you because this is *the truth* that set me free. It was the day I had my epiphany and my life changed in a moment. I was sitting in a classroom with fifty other students studying to become a personal trainer with the Australian Institute of Fitness. It was 1999 and at the time I was still running my video store, feeling like a caged bird, desperate for a way out and a better life. I remember the day like it was yesterday. We were only into the second week of full-time study, learning about physiology and anatomy. Boring for some, *super* exciting for me. However, on this particular day, the first session beginning at 9 a.m., was about personal development. Back then, I'd never heard of personal development and had no idea what it was all about. For some reason I always sat at the front of the class just to be as close to our mentors as possible. I was like a thirsty sponge, soaking in as much knowledge as I could, determined to pass every subject with flying colours. There was no way in hell I was going to flunk *this* class! What I *didn't* know at the time was this topic this day about personal development or self-empowerment, as I like to call it, was about to be the turning point of my life, the day I had my *epiphany.*

That morning we learnt about human behaviour and how each of us had the power to *be, do, or have anything we desired* if we followed a set of universal life success principles. These success principles if implemented, would change our old habits and ways of language, which in turn *empowered* instead of disempowered our thoughts, feelings, and actions, and therefore our results. It was the moment I realized that life wasn't meant to just "happen," and we had to accept whatever came our way, rather life was meant to be whatever *we* wanted it to be. All we needed to do was to change and transform our inner programming and if we did, there was no limit to what was possible. As I sat wide-eyed staring at my mentor, taking in every word, as if she were giving me the numbers to a bank safe, my stomach started churning, my heart started racing while at the same time, tears slowly began welling in my eyes as truth revealed itself.

It was weird. I couldn't control my emotions.

Embarrassed at how my body was responding to her words about the human mind and how we each have total power over our own thoughts, feelings, emotions, habits, behaviours and results in life, it *absolutely blew my mind.* Up till then I, like most people, had been waiting for my "lucky break" in life to show up. Waiting and wishing life was easier or better, instead of wishing *I* was better. Never once did I even *think* to look in the mirror to see who needed to change. Here I was sitting at the front of the room with tears streaming down my face, feeling sick because in that moment I knew that if I wanted a better, more fulfilling life on my own terms, it wasn't up to anyone but *me!*

Shit! Why wasn't I taught this stuff at school?

Up till this moment, I'd spent 33 years of my short, precious life floundering around with a bunch of dreams I wanted to achieve, but with no real plan or direction of how I was going to accomplish them. Nobody except me held the answers to my future and nobody except me had control over my mindset and attitude towards life. The message: *Life doesn't just happen to us unless we allow it* Blinking back tears, I made a decision in that split moment that my life and my mindset would never be the same from that day forward. I felt like a rubber band that had been stretched to capacity and would never go back to being tight and small again. The jolt inside me was so profound I was glued to my seat, holding my breath as my mentor dove deeper and deeper into human behaviour. I was beyond fascinated because for the first time in my life I felt as though the truth was being revealed as she pulled back the curtain on the subject of self-mastery and the power of our habits and thoughts.

The more she talked about life and human potential, explaining things that were new and fascinating to me, the more engrossed I became. Then something happened I can't explain. Over the next two hours, my body calmed down, my mind opened up and I began to feel an overwhelming sense of relief gush over me as the truth that could set me free *finally* dawned on me. I knew then that my life was about to become a magical adventure from this day forward. No more blaming. No more alibies, lies, stories, excuses, or waiting for that lucky break. If it was going to be, it was up to me. I had truly won the lottery of life. I had finally been emotionally set free from the shackles that kept me stuck in a frustrating rut, always wanting more but not knowing how or where to start. As a knowing, more confident smile lit up my face, my mentor happened to look my way, catching the sparkle in my eye and winked at me realizing the "penny had finally dropped" for me. Feeling a mixture of sadness for the lost years, happiness for the joy of the new discovery, and excitement for what was to come, I couldn't wait to re-visit my goals and dreams, as now I knew *exactly how* I was going to achieve each and every one of them!

I will never forget that day and I still hold immense gratitude for the awakening I experienced and how my

AMANDA JANE CLARKSON

life changed and transformed as a result over the coming years. To tell you the truth, I have a tear in my eye right now as I recall this very meaningful story for you. I was broke mentally, spiritually, financially, and personally back then, because I wasn't taking responsibility for my results. Always waiting for my lucky break to come along, yet through empowering myself I soon learnt that *I was the lucky break, and you are too!* As soon as I began living by a new set of empowering life principles, magic began to happen as step-by-step, day-by-day by heading in the right direction, working on my mindset, goals. Dreams I never dreamed would come true, actually became my reality. And this is the *exact* set of life principles I'm going to share with you in a moment, so like me, you too can transform your life like a beautiful butterfly, spread your wings and fly as high as you choose to.

I like to think of a butterfly because its life is short and it's our reminder that life waits for no one or anything. My question for you is, do you wake up each and every day with clear, precise goals and plans just as you would if you were going on a world trip? Are you truly living your full potential and spending your time wisely? How do you *feel* when you wake each morning? Eager for the day and grateful for your life and all that you have? Or are you dissatisfied or fed up with your life and face each morning with dread, knowing you're about to get into a day or go someplace to work you hate? Do you like the person you've become over the years? Or are you pissed at yourself or the world for what life has dished up, like I was before I discovered the answers along with the truth? What do you really want to do with the rest of your life? What are those big chunky goals and dreams you have inside of you

FRUSTRATED TO FABULOUS

that aren't yet real because you don't know how or where to begin making them happen? Are you afraid to go after them and lack the self-belief like most people?

Think about this for a moment: Why is it that some people seem to have it all while others suffer in silence or complain how unfair life is? It's because successful people in any area of life *always* live by a *set of success principles* or a *formula*, as I like to call it, whereas *unsuccessful* people don't. It's *that* simple. My question is, do you live your life by a set of *success principles* or like most, are you spinning your wheels with no idea how to get control and head in the right direction?

If you feel life is passing you by as I once did, if you're unhappy, unfulfilled, angry, sad, lonely, jealous, disappointed, frustrated, and all the other emotions that go with wanting more from life, I have good news for you girlfriend, because it's *never* too late to grow your wings and fly!

Are you ready and willing to live your truth?

Remember, I've walked in your shoes thousands of times. I know how scary and alone you might feel as you step into the life you want but need the assurance and the guidance of someone who's been there before. Someone who not only gets it but lives it!

And has it been easy?

No way, not every time. As if!

Has it been fast?

No, not always.

Has it been frustrating at times?

You bet it has!

Has it been worth it?

You bet it is!

Would I do it again and again and again?

Yes, you bet I would! And still do!

You see, the discovering, learning, growing and expanding, never stops, e*ven if for only small changes*. You'll never go back to being the old version of you because just like with nature, *if you're not growing you're dying*. Step-by-step, day-by-day, following my empowering freedom formula, you'll discover how grand your own life can be. I call it my LIVE NOW Freedom Formula and it's the set of success principles I live my life by, *every single day* without fail. And if you choose to be guided by me and implement these principles, which I'll explain in more detail in a moment, *the priceless gift* that you will receive is that you'll begin to *transform your life in any area you choose to*. The LIVE NOW Freedom Formula is easy to remember, and the transformational success principles are simple to implement as I, and hundreds of my successful students have already done.

Each of the letters in the words "LIVE NOW" represent a success principle, so please stop whatever you're doing right now and write these down in your journal because they're going to give you the life and freedom from frustration you want. Open a new page and as you begin to write out the formula and the principles, it's important that you notice how you feel inside as you do, because these words will become your new blueprint for an empowered and successful life. First of all, I'll go through each letter and give you the

FRUSTRATED TO FABULOUS

success principle to follow, and then I'll go deeper into each one with a brief explanation, so you understand the meaning of each. Some of these success principles will be easy for you to implement right away, others not so easy and may take time. Don't worry. It's normal and part of the process. Remember, one step at a time, one day at a time. And I'll be right with you.

Let's get into it. First of all, below is what each letter of the words "LIVE NOW" represents:

L = Love and let go

I = Imagine

V = Visualize

E = Empower

N = Never quit

O = Opportunity

W = Willing

Now let me briefly explain these success principles, so you can add more words to each of the letters and memorize them, making them your own. Be sure to take notes and remember, also take notice of how you *feel* as you do. Your feelings are your indication of knowing what you want and what you *do not* want. Try to focus your attention on what you do want because *what you think about, you bring about.*

183

Amanda Jane Clarkson

L, Love and Let Go

LIVE NOW: This is the first success principle that is probably going to be the most difficult for a lot of women reading this. You might agree that as women, we take on so many roles in life and often put everything before ourselves and in the end, we're left feeling frazzled, empty, and even angry at how life is working out. The question is, *do you even love your authentic, real self anymore?* Are you constantly beating yourself up internally, never feeling good enough because you compare yourself against everyone else, especially now, as social media is always in your face and you see others living the dreams you have, which makes you feel even worse? Learning to be kinder to yourself and loving who you are is absolutely the first step to experiencing deeper happiness, so that you feel more empowered and inspired to create the life you desire. It's imperative to your future happiness to start noticing from today forward what your self-talk is like and notice just how destructive and mean you can be to yourself, without even realizing the effects.

For instance, remember those little voices inside your head I've been talking about all along? Those are the ones you must listen to and learn to control. Once you begin to consciously take notice of what you say to yourself, like me, you may be appalled at how badly you actually speak to yourself, as I was. The easiest way I've found is for two weeks, track the conversations and self-talk that play in your mind over and over again, and you'll soon see a pattern of language that has become your habitual way of treating yourself. When I did this exercise, I was saddened and shocked at how I spoke to myself in ways I'd never dream of speaking to others! For instance, if I left my car keys on the bench or forgot something important I was supposed to do, I'd call myself a *f****g idiot!* Now, can you imagine saying that to your best friend, or child, or anyone for that matter if they'd done the same? Yet, over and over all day long, your self-talk is probably detrimental to you ever finding happiness.

Now, for your own sake, don't take this advice lightly. Begin the tracking today and write down any destructive words you tend to use repeatedly and promise yourself to stop using them *today*. Even if you must carry a little note pad with you or type them into your phone. Like me, you'll probably be shocked at your own destructive language. Don't worry if at first you feel upset. These words or phrases are habitual and over time if you're serious enough you can learn a new *self-love language* that's incredibly empowering. Once you have your list of words you want to detonate and never say to yourself again, choose new, empowering words, and begin to tell a different story about who you are and what you're made of.

Begin by writing in your journal at least *one hundred things* you like about yourself, taking care to note how you *feel* as you do this exercise. Doing this alone and somewhere you like sitting is best. Maybe light a candle or sit where it's sunny, or run a bath and do it from there, if you want real peace and quiet. The more things you write, the more uplifted and loved you will feel. At first I found this exercise uncomfortable, but as I improved (a glass of bubbles helped me ☺) over time it became a massive tipping point in my life and instead of feeling unworthy, powerless, fearful, unintelligent or uncertain about my own ability to shine, I found myself stepping up in every area of my life.

The next thing I want to talk with you about is the art of *letting go* of the past and learning to live in the now. This can be a touchy subject I know, and don't for a moment think I'm suggesting I have all the answers on this particular topic because I don't. I'm not a professional therapist or anything of the sort, however you can learn from my own experience of going through this process. Guided by numerous mentors over the years, I've learnt the power of forgiveness and letting go of my anger, blame, resentment stories, and excuses by having a clear, defined purpose in life and choosing to live in the now instead of in the past. Practicing this empowering ritual has enabled me to live with eagerness instead of being angry and disappointed in others which kept me trapped in the past for years. In my experience, learning the art of letting go is crucial to your ongoing happiness and it's why I have bundled these two important points together. As Tony Robbins says, "Our emotional habits have profound influence on the way we go through our lives."

The first step is becoming aware of your habitual thoughts and feelings and then making a commitment to change them, if they're clearly not serving you. This process requires dedication and it's why I say change can happen in a moment, however transforming your life and the way you think, often takes time. How much time? Depends on how committed you are! Every day without fail I condition my mind to stay focused on the present and focused on what I want in life, not what I *don't* want. Remember, you get what you focus on so stand guard at the door of your mind. We all have a past—the good, the bad, and the ugly, however it is your personal choice whether you remain living there or let it go and find ways to make peace with it so you can move on. I know that statement may sound like tough love, but living a happy, enriched life whatever this looks like for you is a *choice*. As Tony Robbins says, "It's the small rituals that you do every day that build momentum and, ultimately, lead to massive change." Or as I like to say, a true transformation. And probably like you, I had plenty of excuses and reasons why I couldn't do this or that, but eventually I had to make a decision, as you will. I chose to get help and give up my excuses and stories, because *I wanted life on my terms more than I wanted to be right.*

What about you?

Oprah says, "If you allow your past to define your present, you'll never get to live the life you were meant to live because you're always holding on to what was or could or should have been."

Over time I learnt forgiveness and to let go of the past through educating and empowering myself, and as I discovered more about the natural laws of our universe, I also learnt to let go and surrender my attachment to the outcomes I wanted to achieve after I'd done all I could. I can't control others or situations, but controlling and conditioning my body, mind, and spirit is something I religiously practice daily and so can you. While this may not sound easy—and it isn't—with deliberate practice you'll get stronger mentally, emotionally, and spiritually and your life will turn around as mine did.

Although I'd love to spend hours and hours on this particular life success principle, I'll have to wrap it up here but please don't underestimate the power in the tiny snippet of wisdom I've shared with you so far. It *can* set you free from a life of misery. The great masters say, whatever you hold in your mind on a consistent basis is exactly what you will experience in your life. It's time to be kind, nurturing, and true to yourself and realize that you are worthy of love and achievement in *every* area of your life, *whether or not you believe me right now*. You are a powerful creator and once you learn how to love yourself and let go, you'll discover an inner strength that will be your guiding light to getting the life and happiness I know you want and truly deserve, gorgeous lady.

"In order to grow, you must make a change. With change comes an identity crisis that's really the breaking through of old values and habits."

—Dr. John Demartini

I, Imagine What Is Possible

LIVE NOW: I love this second success principle, because imagination is your gateway to turning the *impossible to possible*. Knowing WHAT you want and WHY you want it, is the key to reaching all your goals and dreams in life. This is where the power of using your imagination comes into play although at first, you must train yourself to being open to new ideas and inspiration for what *could be* possible, before you see the evidence manifested. It is important to know that your limits will be based on your beliefs and conditioning from childhood, however the good news is, if you change your thoughts, you can change your beliefs, which will change your life. Zig Ziglar says, "New information makes new and fresh ideas possible." And even though your little inner-voice will try to play the old record that you're not good enough, not worthy, funny, smart enough, or whatever it says repeatedly, you must train yourself to choose new words through empowering affirmations that help you stay focused on your outcome because you can *be, do* and *have*, anything your heart desires, *if* you believe in yourself.

Right now, imagine yourself as a blank canvas. Vividly think back to when you were younger and felt free from the hassles of life. What did you desire and daydream about mostly? What were those audacious goals you had in your mind that *you swore* to yourself or others that you'd achieve one day?

Who did you want to be?

What did you want to do?

What did you want to have?

Did that *one-day* arrive? Are you living them now? Are you in pursuit of achieving all of them, or at least *some* of them?

Did they get lost along the way when "life" got busy and they didn't seem so important anymore?

Did you share them with others who just laughed, telling you that you were "dreaming?"

Or are they still alive and very real for you and you just don't know how or where to begin?

I get it. We've all been there, and the truth is, it's never too late to realize your potential no matter who you are, or where you've been. And remember girlfriend, all the stories I've shared with you in this guide prove that through the power of imagination and being clear on WHAT I wanted and WHY I wanted it, I have manifested an abundant, free life I truly love living and so can you.

Let me share my secret.

To this day I carry in the back of my phone case my constantly updated list of goals and dreams I want to achieve right down to the specific dates I want to reach them by. I include *what* I want, *why* I want them,

FRUSTRATED TO FABULOUS

who they are going to effect and *how* they will affect others and myself. Right now I am focused on my mission which is to empower you and others like you guiding you to achieving your dreams and transforming your life just as I have done, because I understand the journey you're on and as I mentioned, I've probably walked *thousands of miles* in your shoes in some form or another. You are on my mind morning, noon, and night and I pray or meditate every day that I am successful and so are you. Apart from just praying or meditating though, *I have clear, defined action steps I implement every day,* to ensure I'm on purpose. I get things done and even though there'll be many obstacles along the way, I promise you, I'll never quit on myself or on you.

I read my goals aloud morning and night, so they become part of my being, keeping me inspired and focused even on the days I don't feel like doing anything. It's like magic. When I read them aloud, my physiology changes and I always feel the urge to do something that takes me closer to my outcome. Also, I carry a diary and have a dream board that's full of wonderful pictures to keep me on track. Each night before I go to bed, I write down in order of importance what I want to achieve the following day so when I wake the next day, I know exactly what my day looks like. I control the day, it doesn't control me.

Naturally, like everyone experiences, I have my bad days when shit happens and changes are necessary, however I deal with the issues and step-by-step, day-by-day, I somehow stay on course because I know where I'm headed. Even though the road may twist and wind without notice, if I keep going it makes me feel good at the end of the day. Using a diary, at a glance I can see how my week looks, including all the seven areas of my life:

1. Health
2. Love
3. Money
4. Relationships
5. Personal Growth
6. Happiness and
7. Vocation (my work)

Most importantly above all that, I'm part of mastermind groups which keep me accountable, sharp, open, and growing, beyond my self-imposed limitations. This is the *real gold*, where the magic happens, not only because of the ideas but because others believe in me more than I believe in myself sometimes, which gives me the courage to grow my wings and fly to new heights and beginnings. Now it's your turn to grow your wings, so let me help you get started.

- In your journal write or draw out in absolute details, what your perfect day and life looks like in your mind, remembering you have a blank canvas. Your perfect, average day begins from the moment you wake up, till the moment you lay your head on your pillow at night.

Your perfect *life* is what you imagine in the future and what your goals and dreams are based on. It's super important to have achievable goals along the way so that you don't quit on your long-term dreams. This

FRUSTRATED TO FABULOUS

exercise is paramount and will give you more clarity in deciding WHAT you want, and WHY you want it. You must be exquisitely detailed and include every area of your life. To help you, focus on the seven areas listed above. The reason I say focus on all seven is because as you'd agree, there's no point in having wealth without having amazing health to enjoy it, for example. It's crucial to take note of how you feel as you write because your *feelings or emotions* are your inner guidance system, telling you whether you are focused on what you *do want* or what *you don't* want. The simplest way to know the answer is that if you feel good and you have positive emotions, you're focused in the right direction, and if you feel bad, and you have negative or deflating emotions, you're focusing on what you *don't* want. Be careful here and remember, you get or attract what you focus on so be aware of your thoughts during this process. The great news is that with practice it becomes easier and easier to stay focused on what you want, especially if you write your goals in detail and read them aloud as I suggest. *You can't get it wrong and over time you will notice yourself transforming into the amazing woman you were born to be!*

This can be a very uplifting, exciting exercise for you as you are a bare canvas, which means you can fill it with any pictures you desire. Don't hold back and be as adventurous as you can, tapping into your vivid imagination, saying to yourself these two magic words:

What if…

Girlfriend, *if you can imagine it*, you can manifest it in time, and remember, if others have transformed their lives and made their *impossible* goals or dreams become *possible*, so can you with the right support. You see, one of the biggest blunders people make when writing their goals or dreams is they're not inspiring enough, nor do they consider their WHY. Without knowing your reasons WHY, when adversity strikes—and it will—you may lose your will to get up and keep going, even if you're just an inch away from success. What are you fighting for? Yourself, your kids, your family, your community? Whatever the reasons, they must be strong enough and impact you emotionally when you think about them, or you won't make it! The countless times I failed in life and business would be enough for most people to give up and go back to a life they don't want, however my reasons WHY were so strong and clear that failure paled in comparison to giving up my dreams for a life by my own design. Nothing or nobody was ever going to stop me getting my freedom.

What about you?

What areas of your life do you want to transform and WHY? Your reasons why will be the fuel that will ignite the fire within you to keep going no matter what. Think about *who* you will affect, who you *want* to affect, and how you will *feel about yourself,* once you achieve all that you desire.

Imagine yourself in the moment, right where you want to be.

Can you *feel* the feeling right now?

Does it bring a tear to your eye?

FRUSTRATED TO FABULOUS

Imagine for a moment you have just woken up and it doesn't matter what day it is because you're now living your perfect "normal" day.

What does it look like? What does it feel like? What does it sound, smell or taste like?

Where are you? Who are you with? What will today bring?

Now imagine that for the rest of your life, you get to wake up every day and *be* who you want to be, *do* whatever you want to do and *have* anything you want to have.

How would this way of life *feel* for you?

Wonderful? Scary? Exciting? Possible?

Well, *it is* possible. You can transform your life once you decide to harness the power of using your imagination, getting crystal clear on your WHAT and your WHY and following the LIVE NOW Freedom Formula success principles I'm sharing with you ☺.

One more thing: Be *very* careful that you're constantly focused on *what you do want*; not what you *don't* want for what you think about, you bring about.

"Passion is energy. Feel the power that comes from focusing on what excites you."

—OPRAH

Amanda Jane Clarkson

V, Visualize Success

LIVE NOW: Visualizing success is my third life success principle and it is so powerful and magical, I have butterflies in my stomach as I type this, since I'm living proof that this works over and over again. Seeing in your mind's eye the *having* of what you want in *the now* as though you already have it is where the power sits. In other words, when you think about all the things you want in your life, think about them as though you already have them or live them *now*. Even more powerful is to talk to yourself as though you have already reached your goals and dreams, as it's critical to *believe* before you see the evidence appear, just as the masters of success do. Unless you *believe* you can *achieve* what you want before you actually experience the results, you'll never get there. Please understand the importance of what I'm saying here and don't for a moment think it's "woo-woo" because visualization is exactly how high achievers, such as Olympic athletes, win gold medals. My dream home being one of my biggest goals was a twenty-year vision before it became my reality. For years I cut out beautiful, glossy pictures of Hamptons-style homes and stuck them into my big scrapbook, even down to the street I used to run to for ten years, never knowing that one day it would be the street we built our dream home on.

How amazing is that!?

FRUSTRATED TO FABULOUS

At the time I had no idea how I was going to make that dream come true and in fact, it was hard for me to imagine it, yet I did it anyway. I didn't ever question what my mentor suggested I do, as she was the one with the successful life, not me! I followed the process diligently and the more detailed I was with writing my goals, speaking my goals and adding pictures, the more I began to believe my dreams would one day be my reality. I created so many picture boards of the things I wanted in my life including every area (health, love, relationships, money, personal growth, vocation and happiness). *Why not* do the same? Create your own dream board and stick pictures, or whatever it is that you want to achieve up everywhere and talk to yourself as though you're already living it. The more you say it, the more you believe it and the sooner you'll find a way to live it. Visualize success now and picture yourself dozens of times a day, living your perfect day even if you're nowhere near it yet. It's vital you have something to look forward to that will keep you focused on the now and the future, not the past. To this day, I have pictures and written declarations of what I want out of life which I read aloud twice a day, morning and night, visualizing myself living those goals in the now. The more I read it and see it, the more real it feels.

One of my biggest, and most thrilling goals is my vision and mission of inspiring and mentoring *you* and hundreds of thousands of women along your journey to living your dreams and transforming your life, as I know the path well and understand the importance of having a mastermind of support and guidance to get there. Each day I read out *why* I have chosen this mission and what I want to achieve from doing it. I am clear with most of the details including how I'll do it, and the women who I'd love to support in our mastermind. I can see it, I can feel it, and I speak about it as though it's taking place *now*. Right here, in this moment, I'm your mentor guiding you to life success!

Is this resonating with you at a deeper level of awareness? I sure hope so and I hope you're feeling as excited as I am about your future!

And this is just one vision for my life I'm sharing with you now, however every area of my life is included in my declaration.

"You are more productive by doing 15 minutes of visualization, than from 16 hours of hard labor."

—ABRAHAM HICKS

Now it's your turn. Write the words and collect the pictures that will become your life from today forward. It is best to use as many descriptive words and find as many pictures that represent your goals and dreams as you can, because they'll give you the feelings you're after. Like I did, start a picture dream board. The words and pictures will become part of your psyche. Always remember to be grateful for the now and what is coming to you—*words become things*. It is the natural law. The more emotion you feel doing this exercise, the more you'll *see in your mind's eye and believe* in your ability to achieve each of your goals and dreams. Remember if others have achieved them, so can you. Be sure to include each of the seven areas of life I mentioned above, so you have balance and empowerment over your own life, as you begin to transform into the woman you want to become.

Have fun with this no matter how crazy or far-fetched your goals or dreams may seem today. Never forget that the *impossible* can and will become the *possible* once you take flight, so consistently and persistently take the necessary action steps.

"You are here to live purposely . . . to uncover your magnificent life . . . Let nothing on the face of the earth stop you from fulfilling your inspired destiny. Give yourself permission to shine!"

—Dr. John Demartini

Amanda Jane Clarkson

E, Empower Your Mind, Body, Spirit

LIVE NOW: I love this fourth life success principle because empowering every area of your life—your body, mind and spirit—will be the making of you and I know this because I have been practicing for more than two decades and still do it daily!

"It is in your moments of decision that your destiny is shaped."

—Tony Robbins

Remember the story of the day I had my epiphany and how after hearing the truth I felt that I was *finally* set free? It boiled down to the discovery that I had total control over my attitude towards life and if I educated myself with new, empowering knowledge (nothing I'd learnt at school) my life *could be anything I wanted it to be*. Talk about winning the freedom lottery! Finally, I had the answers I'd been searching for and *now so do you*. Almost every day since then, I have made the time to work on myself by reading, watching, and listening to empowering teachings from different mentors. I have experienced the power of writing and reading goals and dreams aloud, which keeps them alive. (*Not* just passively listening and learning.) Inspired, motivated action has happened as a result and even though life is a journey and *not* a destination, day-by-day I prioritize the goals or things that are most important to me and tick them off as I complete them which helps me stay on target.

- Write down what I just said in this last paragraph if you like, because this is exactly what I do and so can you.

Surround yourself with like-minded people and gain empowering knowledge from those who have walked the path before you. Fly with the eagles in the area of your life you want to change or transform. Get away from the turkeys who try to hold you back and don't want you to change.

The quality of your questions will determine the quality of your life. It truly is your *golden key* to freedom.

My questions for you now, are:

What are the questions you're asking yourself and others about life?

Are your questions empowering or disempowering?

Who are you getting answers from?

Are the people qualified? Do they have the results you're seeking?

Are you seeking and gaining knowledge in all the right places?

Are you in a community of like-minded others who "get you" and want your success as much as you do?

Are you organized and have a diary system that will help keep you focused and accountable?

Are you getting the right answers to your important life goal questions? If yes, fabulous! And if not, keep seeking and you will find them.

And now as you've thought about the areas of your life you want to empower, what is your next step to making it happen? You see; knowledge without applied action is useless, so there are a number of things we can do:

- Write out how you want your life to look in the particular area you want to change, and then decide *how* and *who* will help you get there. Is it a book, a video, an online or offline class, a course, mentor?
- Choose something today and take immediate action. You will feel amazing if you do because it means you're already one step closer to your outcome! Fabulous!

Another idea is to write my following quote out and stick it all over your home, phone, computer, fridge, bathroom, office, car, or wherever you'll see it countless times a day:

FRUSTRATED TO FABULOUS

"Is whatever I'm doing right now taking me closer or further away from my outcome/goals or dreams?"

—AMANDA JANE

This is one of my most favourite and emotive quotes. You can only give one of two answers—Either you are moving closer or you're not! *I love it* ☺ Time waits for no-one. What will you do today that will move you in the right direction? Your answers are all around you. Seek and you must find.

Another one of my tricks you can use is when I get up each morning, I put on my workout gear *whether or not I feel like it,* and head to my home gym. While I work out, I plug into at least an hour of personal empowerment on the TV, my iPad, or on my phone. I watch, listen, and learn from a variety of mentors who have inspired me throughout my journey. This is such an integral part of my day: I never, *ever* read my emails or do any other work until I'm finished working on my body, mind, and spirit for the first hour of the day. By the time I'm done in the gym, my body is energized and feeling fab, plus my mind and inner being is nourished with gratitude, flowing with inspired new ideas and wisdom learnt from the masters of life success. As a result, I'm raring to get into my day and it's still early in the morning! After breakfast I get organized and I'm into my day. Great thing is, because I use a diary and calendar, my mind isn't all over the place and I know how my day will unfold. (Well, most

203

of the time! Yes, shit happens sometimes but I just have to deal with it.) Priorities first and as I work my way down my check list and tick each item off in red, I feel as though I'm accomplishing things worthwhile and that makes me feel satisfied and joyful.

I believe taking care of your body, mind, and spirit is paramount to a fulfilling life so give yourself the gift of time to do so. I remember when I was running Royal Personal Training and was fortunate enough to meet some very wealthy individuals. Some were healthy *and* wealthy, others wealthy *but very* unhealthy. I remember a conversation I had with a gentleman who told me he'd give up his wealth (money in this case) in order to regain his health. Along the way he'd forgotten to take care of his "temple" and over the years it basically crumbled to the point he was in constant pain, which left him feeling broke in *all* ways.

Are you paying attention to the health of your body, mind, and inner being?

Specifically, which of these three areas would you love to transform and be the best version of you?

- Body
- Mind
- Spirit

One of the world's greatest influential philosophers of our time, Jim Rohn says, "Formal education will make you a living; self-education can make you a fortune." Think about this for a moment. It doesn't matter which area of your life you want to change, there are others out there who have blazed the trail before you, right? The truth is, there are others just

FRUSTRATED TO FABULOUS

like you who are already living the goals and dreams you have inside your heart. So what do they know that you don't know? They are *not* smarter than you girlfriend, they just know things that you don't know. *Yet time is on your side.* Success has absolutely *nothing* to do with your age, background, or past. *Nothing!* It has *everything* to do with *all* of the seven LIVE NOW life success principles I'm gifting you here! Success leaves a trail as they say and this is what makes everything possible, doesn't it?

Jim's quote is so powerful, and you can relate it to *every area* of your life because being empowered in all seven areas, will *make you one very fortunate lady indeed, wouldn't you agree?* Jim also says, "Work harder on yourself than you do your job, career or business." I have lived by this quote since 1999 and every day I thank God that I discovered the world of self-empowerment because it gave me the power instead of feeling powerless and it will give you the same if you embrace these teachings.

Are you relating to and enjoying what I'm saying here?

How does this information make you feel? My hope is that it makes you feel ignited with hope and excitement for a brighter future! And it doesn't matter if you've heard this before or not, question is, are you *applying* it to your life? Remember, knowledge without application is useless so here's your chance to write out your a-ha nuggets like wildfire in your journal because there are so many here that if you implement them one by one *your life has to change for better!*

Dr. John Demartini says, "Any area of your life you don't empower, someone else will overpower. The hierarchy of your values determines where you will be in power and overpowered." When I learnt this at one of Dr. Demartini's seminars, it gave me an immediate insight to my own life and the areas I wanted to change or transform. I felt empowered and privileged, realizing that through absorbing and applying new information, I could become the person I wanted to be, *and you can too.*

Looking carefully at your life, what areas would you like to empower or transform? Your health, love, relationships, money, vocation, personal growth, happiness? You can begin with any area of your life, or like me, choose one area that you feel *disempowered* in and make a decision to do something about it today.

It's that simple! Problem is, most people want a new life, but most aren't willing to change themselves. Doesn't make sense does it? You see, if you don't like who you are, or what your life has become, it's up to you to empower yourself through new, applied knowledge and follow the masters who already have the results you want, so you can get there faster and easier. Now I may sound blunt and I get that, and yes, I know I'm repeating myself in a variety of ways, however repetition leads to belief and I am saying all of this with love and for your sake because I know you want a better life, or you wouldn't be reading this, agreed? I care. I really do. However, your body, mind, and spirit are screaming for you to listen to it and find your inner courage and strength to go live those goals you want, or have they been pushed aside?

It's your time and I believe in you. And if that's all you have to hang onto right now, grab it. *I would.*

If it were possible I'd look you in the eye right now and tell you, gorgeous lady, that investing into your self-empowerment is the smartest investment with the highest returns you'll ever make in your life. In fact, it's even smarter than any other investment you'll ever make in my opinion because no matter what life gives us that we don't see coming, your knowledge and conditioned mindset can never be taken away. Just like the time we lost our eBay business in the 2011 Brisbane floods, remember? Without all the work we'd done on ourselves over the years, we'd *never* have rebuilt in such a short time. In those times when all seems hopeless you'll feel the strength, courage, and the will to keep going. Condition yourself and open your mind to gratitude and discover the truth about the universal natural laws of life that will set you free. Remember, it all begins with one step at a time, one day at a time.

Enjoy the journey of your life, it's waiting for you.

"Appreciation is the secret of life. Become a person who appreciates, and you will thrive; you will fulfil your reason for being."

—ABRAHAM HICKS

Amanda Jane Clarkson

N, Never Quit

LIVE NOW: Now let's talk about the fifth life success principle, Never Quit. It might seem obvious in the context of this book, however the truth is that most people quit on themselves and their dreams either before they get started or just inches away from success, for a variety of reasons. This is tragic and unfortunately as an educator and mentor, I've seen it countless times, which saddens me because all the answers are there. What's always lacking though, is an empowered mindset, environment, or determination to keep going after those dreams, no matter what. And most of the time, it comes down to fear, which can be a blessing or a curse depending on how you see it. Fear of rejection, failure, ridicule, criticism, success, loss of love, or even death—Do any of these fears ring true for you?

If your goals or dreams are not *real* or *inspiring* to you, if they're not what *you* want but what someone else wants, there's a high probability you'll want to quit well before you experience success. This is the reason why so many people hate their jobs or their lives. They're fighting day or night for other people's outcomes and not their own.

Any of this *sound familiar?*

While I'm not suggesting quitting your job, career, business or *anything*, I'm suggesting that if you don't have your own goals or dreams, what's it all for? No matter how small or how big they are, just knowing you have something worth fighting for is what counts. You must have something to look forward to that jazzes you and this is why it is critical you write your own "perfect day" in your journal, as it will give you hope and light a flame within you to make the start and keep going. From my experience, you'd be surprised how uplifting this exercise can be for you. My perfect day looks different than Matt's in a few ways, however our values and big dreams are aligned and each afternoon we check in with each other to see how our day was and to plan our next day, which depends on what we accomplished in the day. This kind of communication is vital if you're in business with your life partner or family members and communication is why we *mostly* ☺ have a harmonious, happy, and respectful marriage. And don't for a moment think I'm "luckier" or different than you and I don't have similar arguments, worries, or fears than you, because I do! I'm human and like everyone else I feel the fear too, almost daily in fact. However my dreams are bigger than my problems and myself. This is what keeps me going.

You may recall at the beginning I was reluctant to write this book/guide for you for a number of reasons, which, basically, boiled down to fear. But instead of letting it defeat me, I kept my mind focused on *you* and the importance of my mission to lead and inspire you to live your life. More than once I wanted to quit. I wanted my days back, which I chose to give up for close to six months to write this for you and other women. I wanted my mind to be free of all the worries and stress about how I was going to live my mission as a role model for women and more than a few times I questioned if anyone would even read this book once completed. The self-doubt kicked in so many times, but through sheer will and determination to give confidence and guidance to you and others wanting it, I've pushed through and here we are. If for no other reasons this story changes the way *you think about yourself and what is possible for you*, then it is worth it. You are worth it.

So many of us women don't feel worthy, capable, inspired, intelligent, young enough, old enough, able, beautiful inside or out, pretty, right size, confident, and dozens of other reasons why we never live the life we dreamed of when we were young girls. Like you, I've lived these emotions and the fear of judgment and criticism has made me quit on goals or dreams more than once. And it's why I feel so compelled and passionate as I write this book/guide for you. My gut is in knots knowing you and I are one in the same. What I do not know is if you're surrendering to your fears and stopping yourself from having the life you want. Success in any area of your life requires discipline, resilience, and a healthy, positive attitude to match. The great news is, this stuff can all be learnt, so if you don't have *it* yet, you soon will if you stick with me.

Being accountable to yourself is one thing, however being accountable to mentors or others is even better because most women don't like the idea of letting others down, wouldn't you agree? Today forward, make a pact and adopt your *never quit* mentality and say to yourself at least ten times, every day:

FRUSTRATED TO FABULOUS

🦋 "I will never ever quit on myself again; I am worthy of my goals and dreams."

Saying this in front of your mirror as many times as you can daily will make you into the victor I know you are, no matter how big or small your goals and dreams are. Remember, quitters never win, and winners *never quit!*

"One of the blessings of maturity is that it sometimes brings one greater courage to be truthful, regardless of what those who do not understand, may think or say."

—NAPOLEON HILL

Amanda Jane Clarkson

O, Opportunity

LIVE NOW: The sixth life success principle is *opportunity*, and it's where life's magical rewards await those who seek and find them! Some people call it "luck," though. Oprah says there's no such thing as luck as her definition of luck is simply "preparation meeting opportunity." Whatever you want to call it, from my experience in life, the more *aware* and prepared you are, the more opportunity comes knocking! Have you heard the saying "When the student is ready the teacher will appear?" I love this saying because once you gain clarity on *what* you want, *why* you want it and actually *visualize* the success of achieving it, then you are ready and opportunity will naturally come your way in the form of people, circumstances, disasters, challenges, growth, offers, situations, life lessons, openings, and all sorts of weird and wonderful ways as you train yourself to become more receptive to receiving. ☺

While I don't know your personal story I'm sure you'll resonate with some of what I'm sharing. Where in your life do you see opportunity right now? In your work, community, home, relationships, love, business dealings, church, health, finances, happiness, personal growth?

Now ask yourself this question (which will help give you clarity):

FRUSTRATED TO FABULOUS

🐾 What are my current habits or beliefs that do not serve me (stop you from receiving), and how could I turn each into an opportunity or new belief that will serve me?

This will give you an insight to your *limiting* patterns of thought and which areas of life you want to empower, so your story changes and you no longer feel trapped, frustrated or powerless. This is part of your *preparation,* and as you begin to transform your way of thinking, you will notice more and more that opportunity is always there, it's just how you view it. And if these ideas are new to you, I understand, so take your time and don't be too hard on yourself. Enjoy the experience and know that this one exercise will help you grow stronger and maybe even get you closer to your goals. Be aware, sometimes opportunity is disguised but if you look hard, you'll see, taste, smell, hear, and touch it when you are good and ready. Who knows, maybe your gift or opportunity may come in the form of a problem in some area of your life as it did for me the first time I was asked to speak at a seminar in 2007 and if I didn't there was another lady lined up to take my position, remember? In that same seminar I made a fool of myself and barely got through! The lesson was that I needed to be open and look past my fears and self-doubt, and go out there thinking of the people I would inspire, which completely changed how I was looking at things.

The greatest gifts in life-fulfillment come in the form of opportunity and lessons whether you see them or not, so all you need to do is keep your heart and mind open and be aware. The awesome news is, every day an opportunity will show itself to you and you'll have the choice whether to act on it or not because you will know if it will take you closer or further away from your desires. Prepare yourself girlfriend. There are so many good times ahead and I'm so excited for you *I can hardly type fast enough!*

"Your life does not get better by chance, it gets better by change."

—JIM ROHN

W, WILLING, WHATEVER IT TAKES

LIVE NOW: It is said that the lack of willpower has caused more failure than lack of intelligence or ability. This brings me to my seventh life success principle and it's the one that sets apart the masters and the masses of the world, separates those who live their lives on their own terms from the others who choose to stay in their comfort zone and live a life of misery and defeat. Only *you* have the power to decide which side of the fence you're going to live on and I truly hope with all my heart you have chosen the *masters* side, or you intend to from now on! Dr. John Demartini says, "Most people just get by. They live within their so-called comfort zones and attempt to just fulfil their immediate needs and wants. They eventually end up living or depending on some form of social security. They experience frustration and function from a level of quiet desperation. They do not love what they do, nor do what they love; nor do they let their inspirations run their lives." While this is only a snippet I got from a seminar I attended, the message is loud and clear, wouldn't you agree?

Does any of his statement ring true for you or anyone close to you?

I remember clearly how it hit me like a ton of bricks in my gut and I hope it hits you too. It's a wakeup call for you, as it was for me, to turn your picture board of dreams into your reality and live the life you were meant to. However, it's going to require you to be willing, be disciplined, be committed, and *absolutely* determined to stay focused on your path making sure no one pulls you off course because they will try. Perhaps you have experienced that many times as I have? You begin to make the changes or take action to improve your life and lo and behold your friends, family, or acquaintances start to laugh at your ideas or even ask you. "Who do you think you are?" They tell you, "You're crazy! It'll never work! You're not good enough or smart enough or have the experience," or whatever bullshit they say.

Don't listen to them, even if they're family, and I mean that!

Always remember, empowering yourself isn't about others, *it's about you*. It's about becoming the best version of yourself and impacting others around you in positive ways. You can never be at peace if you try to live someone else's values or ideals. And if you do, you'll wind up miserable. Take it from me, I've been teased, laughed at, and ridiculed to the point where I changed friends or learnt to keep my ideas to myself or only share them with like-minded people. I soon figured out I was far better off leaving the negativity behind because I love my life and so will you. The reason I chose the word "willing" to represent the W in LIVE NOW is because it's the *power of control of the mind to choose one's own actions*. Some might say it is the key to your freedom.

You have the power to control your mind and therefore your actions, if you practice and condition yourself to be aware of your habitual self-talk and learn to trust yourself. This sentence is of *extreme* importance because most people today have given their power away, because they don't want to think or make decisions based on the fear of *positive or negative* consequences. Make the decision to never be a powerless victim of circumstance. You have what it takes to transform any area of your life you choose, and I believe you know it. From a lifetime of personal experience, I know my will and determination to get up and keep going no matter what life gives me has been my key to freedom and it will be yours too. All the stories you've read about my journey so far are just of a few of what I could share with you, but you get the picture. It's up to you.

And one more thing: I would rather go to the end of my days knowing I lived life to the full and realized my dreams with zero regrets rather than spending my last days full of heavy-hearted regret and emptiness, wondering, "What if . . ."

Would you?

Who knows, maybe you've experienced much bigger and more heartbreaking losses than me, however the lesson here is the same. Don't forget, you have a choice, beautiful lady. You were given your gift of life for reasons. Do you remember what those reasons are? Because no matter how big or small your wants or needs may be, if you are *willing* to do whatever it takes by utilizing your will and determination, I promise, you will get whatever you choose if you desire it enough.

Go forward now with your own blessing, and I will see you on the other side.

"Desire backed by faith knows no such word as impossible. It's the desire that transforms the dreams into reality. The more you ask from life, the more you will receive from it."

—NAPOLEON HILL.

FRUSTRATED TO FABULOUS LIFE LESSONS

Okay Gorgeous, it's time to make a nice cuppa, take yourself and your journal to a quiet area for 15 minutes and write in *detail* your top three-to-five take-away *a-has* from my story so far and from the lessons that follow below.

Be Bold.
Be Courageous.
Be Fabulous!

First of all, I trust you've enjoyed this lesson as much as I've enjoyed writing it. There are so many incredible lessons wrapped inside the LIVE NOW Freedom Formula, your head may be spinning! The wonderful thing is, you don't have to walk your path alone, you know that. The cheering and the encouragement from others around you will spur you on through the growth that is just part of the grand adventure we call life! One step at a time, one day at a time, and over a small period of time, you'll be amazed at the changes that can and will take place if you commit *to* yourself. Change can take place in a moment of decision, and transformation is what proceeds.

Now, take a moment and look back through your journal and note which areas of your life you want to change. Then make a decision today to begin. Number each area of your life or a particular goal you want to achieve in order of importance. Then, beside each area or goal, write one thing you can do today that will bring you a step closer to your outcome, even if it's just to make a phone call, book a meeting, have a conversation, write your goals and dreams, start your vision board, begin a program, clean out the fridge, change your wardrobe, ask better questions, or seek smarter answers. Choose *one thing* (from each seven) and promise yourself to act today and you will have begun your transformation to being more empowered and the woman you want to be.

Are you up for it?

Are you ready, willing and able?

If you are, I'm excited for you!

Take comfort in knowing that every day people all over the world are living their lives with fulfillment and you can too. Great examples of willpower and an attitude of *willing to do whatever it takes* are inspired by two of my favourite TV shows I watch while working out in my home gym. They are *Shark Tank USA* and *MasterChef Australia*. I love both of these shows because not only are they incredibly inspiring, but here you have everyday people from all walks of life turning the impossible into the possible. All of these people have goals and dreams and are determined to make them become reality. They know *what* they want, *why* they want it, and they all believe in themselves. They have the will, a positive attitude, and are willing to do whatever it takes as they eagerly sell themselves and their products to their mentors and the world. They are all living their dreams, turning their dreams into reality, waking up inspired to go do what they were born to do, just like we were all meant to do, wouldn't you agree? They surround themselves with leaders, with others on the same journey, and they fuel their dreams through *Love, Imagination, Visualization, Empowerment, Opportunity, Will and they Never Quit* on themselves ☺

What is the lesson here?

Surround yourself with greatness and find inspiration from your heroes if you can't find it within yourself just yet. There is love, help, support, and opportunity all around you. All you need to do is open your heart, open your mind, and listen carefully to your inner guidance. Trust in your natural, God-given magnificence and go for it, Gorgeous!

Okay, you've been on a journey with me inside this book. You've seen where I have stumbled and where I have succeeded. You've seen me in times of despair and in times of joy. And I've revealed my LIVE NOW Freedom Formula, so you too can dare to live the life of your dreams. But this book is not over yet. There is one more chapter to go. And it could be the most important chapter in this whole book.

Are you ready for it?

Then turn the page.

FREE GIFT

www.gdaygorgeous.com/webclass

[12] THE BUTTERFLY EFFECT

"What you think, you become. What you feel, you attract. What you imagine, you create."

—BUDDHA

IF YOU WERE GIVEN the news today that you had less than twelve months to live, and you were granted a magic wand in order to have the life you wanted, do anything you wanted to do, become anyone you wanted to be, and have anything your heart desired, what would you choose?

The life you live *now*?

Or the life you *want to* live?

If you're open to it, I'd like you to come on a mini-adventure with me for just a moment or two. Make sure you're alone and with *no* distractions. Turn off your phone and sit somewhere quiet and comfortable with your journal in hand if possible, and if not stay with me anyway. Now, with an open mind and heart, read carefully and think deeply on what I'm about to share with you. You see, the final chapter of this book isn't about me, although I'll share one last story with you, it's about you. And as you've probably worked out by now, nobody really cares about your life, goals, and dreams as much as you do, so please allow me for a moment to be your mentor here, because I understand what success looks, feels, smells, sounds, and tastes like, and I want you to know the same.

Imagine if together we could create a grand, new chapter of your life, a grand new chapter that represents who *you really are* and *what you want* your life to look like in every single area in detail, beginning today. All I ask is that you put aside any limiting beliefs around what I'll share with you in this final chapter for *what is possible* for you. Because *I swear to you*, this is the most important lesson of all because you can be the cause of massive change not only within yourself, but within your family and others you surround yourself with.

What if . . .

However, before I get into that, I'd like to explain the reason I chose "The Butterfly Effect" as the name of this final chapter and what it has to do with you. (Actually, there are two reasons, and I'll get to the second one later in this chapter.) The story of how butterflies are created by nature is extremely unique and worth understanding, as the butterfly represents a *true symbol of change and life transformation.* It symbolizes what we go through when we choose to make change, leaving the past behind, to live in the now, while we make plans for a brighter future. And I'm talking about, real change and a real transformation process, not just surface changes that rarely last. Let me briefly explain the meaning behind why I chose the majestic butterfly as a symbol and reminder of how short and precious your life is. In a butterfly's short life cycle, there are four stages. In the second stage when the eggs hatch, the caterpillar emerges. It eats constantly, growing and expanding quickly, although its outer skin doesn't stretch or grow. In order for the caterpillar to grow, it undergoes a process called *moulting* where it *sheds the outgrown skin several times as it forms.* The third stage of a butterfly's life is remarkable. As soon as the caterpillar has finished growing to their full length and weight, they form themselves into a *pupa,* also known as a *chrysalis.* From the outside, it appears as though the caterpillar is resting, but *on the inside* there is a process in action with a *change rapidly taking place.* Within the chrysalis, the old body parts of the caterpillar are *undergoing a miraculous transformation known as metamorphosis* to become the beautiful parts of the butterfly that will soon emerge. The tissues, limbs and organs of the caterpillar have changed, ready for the final stage of the butterfly's life cycle. Finally, when the caterpillar has done all it's changing and transforming

FRUSTRATED TO FABULOUS

inside the pupa, the butterfly is ready to emerge from the chrysalis.

As the butterfly emerges, both of its wings are soft and folded against its body, as it had to fit inside the pupa. After the butterfly rests, it begins to pump blood into its wings to get them working and flapping. It can take around three to four hours for a butterfly to master flying. And then, the fourth stage, the beautiful butterfly is ready to spread its wings and fly, in search of a new mate and to begin the process all over again. They do not waste a moment of their precious life, *they live in the now*. Their purpose in nature is to pollinate and carry pollen from plant to plant, helping fruits, vegetables, and flowers produce new seeds. They are said to be *free spirits* in their flight and *lack constraints*. Most adult butterflies only live for one or two weeks with the average lifespan of just one month. Only the Monarch Butterfly lives for up to nine months.

Think about this story for a moment if you will. It's a brief insight to how the magnificent butterfly is formed. I love this story and I love butterflies. In fact, whenever I see them flying around I always stop to watch them. I find their colour, beauty, and grace absolutely mesmerizing. However, the reason for the name of this chapter, "The Butterfly Effect," has been chosen as it represents a true transformation, which is what's necessary, if *you* want to see massive change in your life that is long-lasting.

To be honest, before I wrote this book/guide for you, I'd never really thought too much about a butterfly's lifespan, however in the context of this book, and all that you've learnt wouldn't you agree a butterfly is a perfect reminder of how precious and short your life is and the fact that you're here to make the most of every moment life is *gifting* you?

Imagine if *you* only had a year to live?

Would you choose to *be* anyone other than who you've become?

Would you *do* anything different than you're doing now?

Would you *have* a different life than the one you're currently living now?

Would you say that you're *truly living…now?*

Or are you the one that's constantly getting *ready to live*, but never *really living?*

Are you where you *thought* you'd be in all areas of your life right now?

Are you living the health, wealth, and personal fulfillment you've always wanted and absolutely deserve?

And now my question for you is this:

If you had *just one year to live*, would you like to write a grand new chapter of life, beginning today, and transform your life into what you want and deserve, or would you carry on as you are?

Does this question get you as emotional and thoughtful about life as it does me?

Please know, I'm not here to point or judge. I'm no different than you are but before I get to the second reason why I chose The Butterfly Effect as the name

FRUSTRATED TO FABULOUS

of the final chapter, I have one last life story to share with you that profoundly impacted my life, making me realize just how precious life and time are. A couple of years ago we came face to face with Mother Nature in an incident that frightened me to the core. It was a wakeup call you might say. Here's what happened. In late August 2016 Matt and I were heading south on the Pacific Ocean on our motor boat which is actually called LIVE NOW. We were returning home after a six-week boating trip in the stunning waters of the Whitsundays of Australia's Barrier Reef. It was whale season, which is the time of year when the whales head north to breed in the warmer tropical waters of the Pacific. As we were heading south, the whales, some with their baby calves in tow, were beginning their long journeys home. It is a magical time of the year and to watch them migrate is a fabulous experience.

I must admit, the beauty and thrill of being able to head north on our boat alongside the whales six weeks prior, watching them up close and seeing the calves alongside their mothers, is what I often call a spiritual or enlightening experience. Whales are as massive and majestic as they are breathtaking in grace and beauty. I felt blessed to be in their presence. We saw hundreds of whales, baby calves, dolphins, turtles, and all sorts of stunning tropical fish, reefs, and islands you can only see from a boat. Life was good.

As we were driving the boat home southbound this particular day, Matt, who's the captain of course, needed to quickly duck downstairs. (The boat had a fly bridge, which means upstairs area for driving.) It was around 4 p.m. and we were at least two hours away from docking as the sun slowly began to set over the west of the hills. As always, if Matt left the helm, I would take over and steer or watch carefully even if the boat was set on autopilot, which it was this day. Within moments of Matt heading downstairs a massive whale came to the surface of the water on the left-hand front of the boat. The sight of this massive mammal, which hadn't noticed we were on his path as he surfaced for air, frightened me to the point I thought I was going to throw up in fear right then and there. Instantly I jerked the steering wheel down hard to the right to avoid hitting it, which was just a natural instinct. The boat was sixty-five feet long and at this length you really notice any severe steering action. As the vessel veered sharply to the right terror rose in my throat. The waves were high and rolling so going against them made it feel as though we were going to roll, especially as we were so high out of the water.

I screamed in sheer fright and I heard Matt holler out to me as he flew up the stairs to see what had happened and to take over the helm. I was shaken badly and as Matt quickly took control of the boat he made a decision to push on the throttle and get to the dock as fast as possible. Neither of us had expected these many whales to be in our path and we just wanted to get out of their way as fast as we could! No more than ten minutes later, as we sped towards the river mouth where a safe port was waiting, the boat all of a sudden lost power in one engine and within moments it practically came to a stop. We had no idea what had happened, all we knew was we had no steering power as the boat slowly began to go around in circles running on one engine. It was an eerie feeling being out in the ocean, with almost no engine power, knowing there were whales everywhere. I didn't like it one bit.

FRUSTRATED TO FABULOUS

The sun was quickly sinking to the west as Matt phoned our marine mechanic for help. They went over a number of scenario's but nothing we did would restart the second engine. Forty minutes later we were still floating at sea with almost zero steering power, the sun was setting quickly, whales were everywhere, Matt had gone quiet (thinking) and I felt like shitting myself. When Matt went quiet, I knew we were in trouble. The life raft bag was behind us ready *just in case*, never for a moment believing we'd consider opening it, let alone using it—God forbid! One thing about Matt, he's extremely sensible and safety is always top of mind when we're out boating. I asked what his plan was and because this problem had never occurred in all the years we'd been boating he was going over the scenarios in his mind before he decided. He began running me through our practiced process in the "unlikely event" of an emergency, which made me panic even more. As the sun sank over the west, so did my heart and I have to say it was one of the most frightening nights of my life.

Matt had to put all of his strength on the steering wheel, just to stop the boat from going in circles as we slowly limped along. We had no choice but to limp the boat back to the port on one engine, which was now going to take about four hours in the pitch black. I felt like crying, as my thoughts raced taking in everything around me and deciding that if we had to get off this boat for any reason at all, I'd take nothing except my life jacket and myself. It's funny how your mind works under immense pressure, when you're not trained for it in this particular instance, and for some reason I went downstairs to put on my gym clothes thinking to myself that if anything were to happen, I wanted to be wearing clothes that were easy to move in. I kept telling myself everything would be all right but all I could think about was what if we hit a whale and damaged the boat or worse, put a hole in it? I know this sounds dramatic, but at the time it was very real for me. I was thinking to myself, *Dear God, is this it?*

I went back upstairs to be with Matt not giving a single moment of thought to *anything* but us and the life we'd lived. All the material possessions we owned didn't matter, but in the hours that followed as we limped the boat back to the dock mostly in silence, so Matt could concentrate and control the steering that had almost completely locked up by now, I began to think about my life and what was *truly* important to me. The question I ran through my mind being, if this *were* the last day of my life would I have any regrets? I am grateful to say my answer was a heartfelt, *no regrets*. I have so far lived a full, adventurous life with so many experiences I could fill a few more books! From leaving home at 16 years of age, my life has seen many twists and turns but all leading me to where I am today. Mostly happy, fulfilled, and on purpose doing what I love, and *loving* what I do.

Eventually, we made it back to the dock around 8:30 p.m. in total darkness, almost five hours after we'd lost an engine. I'd never seen Matt so exhausted, but he held himself together, never letting me witness the fear he also felt because he didn't want me to panic anymore. Thankfully there were some people able to assist us and over a glass of wine hours later, Matt shared that he'd been thinking similar thoughts to me that day, thinking about the twenty years we'd shared, all the dreams we'd shared and had mostly lived, and

FRUSTRATED TO FABULOUS

the dreams he hadn't yet realized but was working towards, all similar thoughts to mine racing through his mind on that long, dark journey back to the dock. Thankfully, like me, he said had no regrets either and that this day was a great reminder of how short life is. *He told me that night that he was never going to waste his time doing anything he didn't want to do for the rest of his life.* I believed him, and he stayed true to his word to this day.

Life is full of surprises and who knows, maybe we needed to gain some new perceptive on life and were given the opportunity in the way of adversity. My hope is that you see from my final story here that my intention is to get you thinking about your life, too. It's to remind you that time waits for *no one* or *anything* and if you're reading this and you've stayed with me throughout this journey, chances are high you want to live your life with no regrets either. And, as I've mentioned a few times now, it's never too late to make your decision and your commitment to begin today. You *can* have a life by design whatever that looks like to you, but you need a plan and a formula that you can implement for the rest of your days.

You can see from sharing just a tiny snippet of how I live my life according to my LIVE NOW Freedom Formula, that there is an *ocean of knowledge, wisdom, and gifts of life* I would love to share with you. But let me share with you the second reason I called this chapter the Butterfly Effect. Once you begin to make these small changes in your life step-by-step, day-by-day, you'll begin affecting others around you, because just like a butterfly does, you will have a positive impact far greater than you may realize, just from changing your mindset, your actions and your results. Imagine how your life could be so much brighter and how this will affect your family, your children, and loved ones. Imagine the positive impact you'd have on your friends as they witness you morphing into the person you want to be and slowly but surely getting a life you always wanted. Imagine how proud of yourself you will feel and how others will look up to you when you begin to tick off your wish list sooner than even you thought possible. And imagine what it would be like to wake up each morning eager for the day ahead, no matter which day of the week it is, because you're finally *living* some of those dreams you've had for years, maybe even decades.

Just like a butterfly, which enriches the world by spreading pollen of flowers and vegetables, you too can enrich the lives of your friends, family and community, all because you decided to make a decision and commit to yourself.

This guide is the first step towards creating a global movement, remembering that in nature the whole ecosystem is enriched by the butterflies going from flower to flower, spreading precious pollen that enables plants to germinate and grow for future generations. You too can help your friends, family, and community to become better off by helping to create a global movement of women who are constantly moving towards empowering themselves, living their goals and dreams, and spreading the message of hope.

And if you're thinking, *Get real, Amanda! This is all hogwash!* Think again! I am living proof that it doesn't matter who you are or where you've come from, your age, background, or education. It's all irrelevant! I left

FRUSTRATED TO FABULOUS

home to live by myself at sixteen years of age, with nothing but a few belongings and a heart full of dreams. Today, I am a self-made woman in my *very* early fifties feeling more fabulous now than when I was in my thirties! I'm a best-selling author, entrepreneur, international speaker, coach, and mentor to thousands of people all over the world through my books, education programs, live seminars, workshops and community. I live my life happily by design, doing what I want, whenever I want, and with whom I want. I'm healthy, fit, and still in love with my husband after being together for twenty-two years. I have great relationships with family and friends and my mentors keep me focused and on course with my mission. More importantly than that, it's important for you to know that I'm authentic and actually *walk my talk and always leave the B.S. at the front door where it belongs!*

I'm not sharing any of this private stuff with you to brag, it's not my style. I share for no other reason than to stir something deep inside of you—your God-given guide telling you that *if Amanda can do it, so can you!* Gorgeous lady, just imagine your newfound inner power and freedom and whom you could affect, once you become the best version of you.

When I started out, I had no mentor and no clue how or where to begin to make my dreams come true. I had to learn through life experience and to tell you the truth, I would rather have had a guide and a mentor at any cost. It was hard and lonely by myself. You, on the other hand, won't need to go through some of those bloody *awful* life lessons that I did, and I know you've already had plenty of your own awful and challenging life lessons. However it's knowing how to channel that experience along the way that can help the positive change you may be seeking. And if you allow me to guide you, you can *lean in* on my experience and shortcut your journey to authentic happiness, whatever it means to you. Only caveat is, please don't hope that I'll sugar coat what it takes to become successful in different areas of your life, it's not my truth and if you're looking for a quick fix, I'm probably *not* your gal. There's no such thing anyway.

And although change can happen in a moment of decision, as I've said before, a true transformation takes time. And time, if spent wisely, can bring you the greatest gifts of all.

Throughout my many years of mentoring, coaching, speaking, and being a role model to stay-at-home mothers, corporate ladies, empty nesters, baby boomers, and amazing women from all ages and walks of life who also wanted to reach their own goals and dreams, the *biggest frustration* most of them faced was not knowing what to do or where to begin making change. Most women just felt stuck. I could relate easily because it was how I felt for years and years as I bumbled through life, always looking outside myself to justify my results. And then, as you might recall, I had my epiphany and wake up lesson in 1999, sitting in a classroom studying to become a personal trainer. From that day forward, I made a promise and commitment to myself that I would become empowered through education and with mentors who could help me become the woman I wanted to be. From the moment I made that decision, I did what *all successful* people in life do—I took *instant massive action* and as a result I have *never once* looked back wondering what could have been.

Now as we come to the end of this book and guide that I have *passionately* written for you, you've seen how important it is to continue learning and growing, so you get the best out of your life. We've been on a journey together, a journey I would love to continue with you. That's why I invite you to join me on a very special and free web class. In this web class, I'm going to share more with you on my LIVE NOW Freedom Formula. I want to give you more direction. I will give you steps to follow and tools to guide you, so you can implement these success principles into your own life. This way, it'll be so much easier for you to take action and start living the life you so thoroughly deserve. This is just the beginning. A new life awaits you if you dare to dream and dare to take action.

I'm looking forward to sharing more of my wisdom with you and to mentor you further, so you can change and transform your life. I'm getting excited just thinking about it. If you feel this book has given you hope, inspiration, and the courage to go out and live the life you want, then this web class is for you.

Let's continue this exciting journey together.

FREE GIFT

www.gdaygorgeous.com/webclass

FREE GIFT!

THIS BOOK is just the beginning of our time together. I have another special gift for you, gorgeous—a gift that will clarify the lessons in this book and give you a better idea on how to live your life by design, not default. Introducing my…

LIVE NOW Freedom Formula
Web Class

During this online presentation, I go deeper into my LIVE NOW Freedom Formula, so you too can transform your life and live with more confidence, choice, and freedom. Based on over two decades of life lessons and tens of thousands of dollars invested in the best mentors from around the world, this web class

FRUSTRATED TO FABULOUS

gives you the power to take control of your life and design the life you truly deserve. You'll discover...

- The easiest way to banish negative self-talk and fill your life with hope and joyful expectations! (You'll see how to let go and love yourself for who you are.)

- How to stay on track every day no matter what life throws at you. (Never get overwhelmed again.)

- The simple exercise that turns your dreams into reality. (This is an important part of your transformation.)

- How to feel empowered every minute of every day. (Gives you confidence and certainty in an uncertain world.)

- An important element in your success journey you must master. (Makes you unstoppable.)

- How to be effective not just busy. (A powerful exercise that gets things done.)

- Unlock the power of your mind and take control of your thoughts, habits, and actions. (This is where your true transformation begins.)

And so much more! So let's continue this grand new adventure together. This web class is the perfect companion to this book and gives you extra clarity on transforming your life. To register for this FREE web class, simply go to this link:

www.gdaygorgeous.com/webclass

Praise

"Well, you changed my life today. Your content-rich presentation was brilliant. The depth of knowledge you have and the excitement and enthusiasm you brought to the room was palpable. Thank you!"

—Rebekah J.

"Thanks Amanda, amazing content as always. Appreciate your incredible intelligence and Tassie wit."

—Bernadette L.

"Amanda, your passion and your wisdom are amazing, and we are so lucky to have you help us all! . . . It's changing my life and was the reason I doubled down and got my product live. You're awesome!"

—Cameron B.

FRUSTRATED TO FABULOUS

"You deliver amazing content Amanda. You share it with so much passion and take pride in what you do. Your personality is contagious, and you leave a room filled with so much energy. Thank you for your humour. Thank you for sharing your knowledge with us"

—MANU R. P.

"You are truly inspirational, thoroughly enjoyed your presentation today. I learnt so much and can't thank you enough for your honesty, exceptional detail and wisdom that you shared today."

—MARGIE M.

"Amanda, your presentation was a key highlight for me today and sharing your real experience reflects who you are and what you want out of your students. I saw how passionate you were up on stage and I LOVED IT!"

—RATHA R.

"Thanks Amanda for sharing your wisdom with us! Loved your presentation, your energy, and your passion!"

—JENNY L.

"I don't think you have any idea of the empowering, emotional effect you had on me and my life personally. Your words have more of an effect on people than you get credit for. It took a while to set in. I was a bit of a cranky pants, and I left your seminar on the Gold Coast two years ago with the song, "Magic" in my head. It nearly made me cry.

"Amanda's advice of one hour in the morning of hammer time exercise and simple, effective words allowed me to believe where I hadn't dared to dream before. It was about empowerment. I can do this, and no one is going to stop me. No one has the right to stop me. I was unsure at first, but you both are the real deal."

—CAMERON N.

"You rock, Amanda! Your passion, energy, and enthusiasm are infectious! Thank you for your commitment to students!"

—FAZILA E.

"You were amazing today. Thank you for imparting such a wealth of knowledge and experience to help us all from mistakes we don't need to make. You're a treasure!"

—KERI L.

FRUSTRATED TO FABULOUS

"That was an incredible, world-class presentation and performance. I could sit through 100 more. Thanks Amanda!"•

—JAMES C.

"Trustworthy, authentic, kind, considerate, honest, empowering, knowledgeable—These are just a few words that accurately describe Amanda. She is extremely generous in sharing the vast amount of knowledge they have learnt over the past years on how to successfully create and run an online business."

—JULIE C.

"Just want to say thanks for what you are doing. If you give somebody a fish, you feed them for a meal but if you teach how to catch fish you feed someone for life. You are teaching people to fish and maybe you don't realize it but you are feeding a nation for life."

—ANDRE AND LEONIE

"Dear Amanda, I am brand-new and trying to absorb this incredible wealth of information like a thirsty sponge. I have seen you speak now on several occasions and been through a full box of tissues listening to your story, thinking about my own, and seeing where you have gone and what you have achieved. I just wanted to tell you that you are truly inspirational and on my bucket list now is to meet you some fine day. Thank you again for your enthusiasm, your willingness, and your true desire to help new starters learn this amazing business. What you offer is not only your course materials but of yourself as well. It's priceless and I am very grateful."

—ELLY L.

"Amanda has changed my life and my daughter's life. Your seminar opened our eyes and we've never looked back. Everything we learnt we implemented. All parents want the best for their children, but to give her self-belief and the know-how to achieve her dreams is priceless. Amanda has inspired me and helped me along the journey. Thank you, Amanda, for the inspiration. Your own story shows that you have been there and walked this same path to success. I cannot thank you enough!"

—CECILIA I.

"Amanda I'm in. Love learning from you as you have walked the walk and are so open and genuine about it. I have recently been reading books from Robert Kiyosaki and Napoleon Hill for personal growth and I class you as one of these masters."

—CHERIE T.

FRUSTRATED TO FABULOUS

"Amanda, thank you. You make such a difference!"

—ANNETTE L.

"I can't get enough and so grateful for your teachings."

—SONIA N.

"I just wanted to share that what you are teaching is really landing. So many things are really changing for me. My mind is shifting! It's been exciting. Stacks going on but I can really feel a new mindset. Thank you and I know it's only the beginning of the journey but super exciting."

—HELEN D.

"We had the privilege of hiring Amanda Clarkson to coach us with our business a few years ago. She went absolutely over and above with her training. Amanda has amazing knowledge, skill, and wisdom with starting, growing, and expanding your business, carving years off of having to figure it out for yourself and teaching vital skills to your success with personal growth. I was blown away with the value she brought each session. I absolutely love Amanda and am forever grateful for how she has helped us to transform our lives."

—CASSY M.

AMANDA JANE CLARKSON

"I have just started your program and I truly feel like you are speaking to me. It is so amazing, and exhilarating and I am glued literally! It makes so much sense and I am truly very thankful for this knowledge that you are imparting. Half way through stage one I felt compelled to just say *thank you*!"

—PAPPY S.

About the Author

AMANDA JANE is a bestselling author, entrepreneur, inspirational speaker, and mentor who has shared the stage with prominent world-renowned speakers and business leaders such as Tony Robbins, Ita Buttrose, Robert Kiyosaki, and Dr. John Demartini.

Amanda left school at 16 and has had 33 jobs and 14 businesses over the past 25 years. Since 2007 she has mentored and deeply impacted thousands of people with her business, and with her empowering education programs and life success formulas. Amanda's vision is to inspire, empower, and lead women to live their dreams creating a life they truly love and deserve. She's living proof her LIVE NOW Freedom Formula works.

For more information on Amanda Jane visit her website:

www.gdaygorgeous.com

Acknowledgements

MY SUCCESS, AS I KNOW and live it today, would not be possible without the many, incredible mentors I've had the privilege to learn from, since my journey of self-empowerment and the hunger to know how to live on my own terms began in 1997 after reading *Rich Dad, Poor Dad* by Robert Kiyosaki.

All of the stories and my LIVE NOW Freedom Formula I share with you in this guide are from my own personal experiences, however the lessons I give you are based on my own results and what I have learned from many great teachers, mentors, and life itself. These empowering success lessons are based on my own results, experience, and the universal laws of nature and attraction, which these days are thankfully talked about and embraced globally. Some of my mentors have mentored me personally, others from books, DVDs, CDs, podcasts, videos, audios, courses, and seminars. Without my many and varied mentors, some of whom have passed, I know my life as I live it now would not have been possible. Either way, the life success lessons I have gathered, implemented, and lived as a result, have shaped me into the woman I have become today—happy, fulfilled, prosperous, on purpose, and experiencing a world abundant with possibility.

For this, I am humbled and grateful far beyond these few words. I thank you all from my heart: Napoleon Hill, Earl Nightingale, Abraham-Hicks, Jim Rohn, Dr John Demartini, Tony Robbins, T. Harv Eker, Robert Kiyosaki, Brian Tracy, Bob Proctor, Zig Ziglar, Oprah, Ita Buttrose, John Assaraf, Mark Sneddon, James Allen, Dale Carnegie, Michael Gerber, Mylene, Maureen Hughes, Rodney Miles, Adam Hudson, Rick Cowley and of course, my rock and the true love of my life, sexy hubby Matt Clarkson. You believed in me even when I often doubted myself. You have always, in all ways, allowed me the space and the encouragement to live my life exactly as I wanted and to see me bring my gifts and wisdom to others. For this I love you even more.

And of course, never forgetting so many others who have made my life even more fabulous by being part of it. My gorgeous, cherished friends who I laugh endlessly with, my family, Mum and Dad who continue to take care of our home and pets, so we have more freedom to do the things we love, my current and past students and staff members Carmel, Genta, and Grace who believed in us, and our education.

And now, *you,* my new friend.

I love and appreciate you all. You all have helped shape me and my life and as a result I feel grateful to be alive every day!

FRUSTRATED TO FABULOUS

Amanda Jane Clarkson

FRUSTRATED TO FABULOUS

AMANDA JANE CLARKSON

CPSIA information can be obtained
at www.ICGtesting.com
Printed in the USA
LVHW040538120423
744131LV00009B/438